Turbulent Teens of Panicking Parents

Also by Jeenie Gordon

There's Hope after Divorce (Formerly *Cementing the Torn Strands: Rebuilding Your Life after Divorce*)

If My Parents Are Getting Divorced, Why Am I the One Who Hurts?

Christmas 97
With much love from
Jenn

Dear Auntie Gaye,

I loved this book and I thought you might enjoy it as well. I love you and keep you in my prayers...

Turbulent Teens of Panicking Parents

Jeenie Gordon

1 Peter 5:8 "Be self-controlled and alert. Your enemy the devil prowls around like a roaring lion looking for someone to devour."

ohn 10:10 "The thief (devil) comes only to steal and kill and destroy; I have come that they may have life, and have it to the full," said Jesus.

ESUS in Matthew 11:28 "Come to me, all you who are weary and burdened, and I will give you rest."

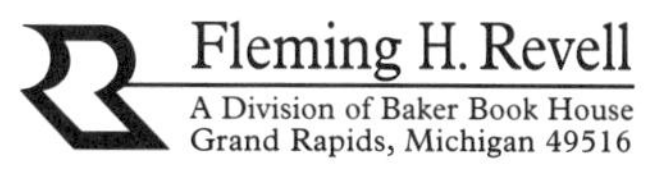

Fleming H. Revell
A Division of Baker Book House
Grand Rapids, Michigan 49516

go to back cover →

Published by Fleming H. Revell
a division of Baker Book House Company
P.O. Box 6287, Grand Rapids, MI 49516-6287

Printed in the United States of America

Library of Congress Cataloging-in-Publication Data

Gordon, Jeenie.
Turbulent teens of panicking parents / Jeenie Gordon.
p. cm.
Includes bibliographical references.
ISBN 0-8007-5620-7 (pbk.)
1. Parent and teenager. I. Title.
HQ799.15.G67 1997
649'.125—DC21 96-49108

All names of persons whose stories are shared have been changed, as have their situations, in order to protect their privacy.

For current information about all releases from Baker Book House, visit our web site:
http://www.bakerbooks.com

To
Ethel Mayola Olson West

She had a sense of humor that wouldn't quit
And a personality that went with the red hair.
Poverty was her companion, but so were her three kids.
She sewed for other people to provide a living,
Yet the song was always there (a bit off key).

Cancer took her young, vibrant spirit away much too soon.
The three kids grew up to be vital Christians—one a minister.

Materially she was a pauper—yet the richest lady I have ever known.

Thank you, Lord, for my mom!

Contents

Acknowledgments

Thank you to

Bill Petersen (Revell) who believed in my work and encouraged me during three publications. A true mentor.

The support staff at Baker Book House and Fleming H. Revell—a great team for me.

Students at Glen A. Wilson High School, whose stories have been changed beyond recognition, but whose lives touched mine.

Sharon West, my sister (in-law), who went to live with Jesus a few weeks before this book was published. Always honest, supportive, inspirational and encouraging—fun and pretty, too. Whom I will always miss.

Introduction

Parenting an adolescent is a tough job!

"I can't believe him," the well-dressed, concerned parent in my office screeched. "He was super when he was a little kid. Don't know what's happened to him. It seems like when those hormones kicked in, he changed overnight. He's driving me crazy."

As a high school counselor of nearly twenty years as well as a therapist in private practice, I've worked with over eight thousand teens. Plus, I've raised my own.

Teen years are not always easy, and sometimes they're downright horrid. It's scary. Normal parents dread the onset of teenage years.

But this book is about hope. It will encourage you to hang in there, practice good parenting techniques, and feel confident in the future. It's also practical.

At the end of each chapter is a section called "Coming to Grips." It consists of exercises that will help you put the chapter information into practice. This book will tell you how to:

talk to your teen,
set limits,
discipline,
get your teen through school,
let go,
build self-esteem,
deal with alcohol, drugs, and sex.

I will let you in on things your teens may never tell you themselves.

So, here we go!

1

"Listen Up, Kid—I'm Talking!"

The evening was typical. I was trying to get dinner on the table—watching the boiling pots and stuff in the microwave, browning rolls in the oven—desperately hoping to pull it all together.

Minutes before I'd received one of those "Congratulations! You've won something" telephone calls. I was annoyed. *Get real*, I thought.

The dog was chasing a bird and barking her head off. A blaring T.V. added to the confusion.

All the while my junior high daughter had been talking, talking, and talking. *Like I need this*, I thought. Tipping my head toward her, I painted on an "Oh, how interesting!" smile. I even inserted some "uh-huhs." *Hey, I'm coming off great*, I reasoned. Finally, I mentally tapped into the conversation and decided it would be a good time to ask her a question about the topic.

She exploded. "You weren't listening to me, were you? I just told you that. You *never* listen to me."

My first response was to defend myself. "I was listening to you, my dear," I almost answered. I chose instead to say, "Kathi, I'm sorry. I apologize to you because I wasn't listening. But, if you run it through again, I promise I'll listen this time."

Reluctantly, she did.

A few days later, I pondered the event. *How can I learn to listen?* I wondered. *Sit on the floor.* The thought thundered through my mind. As I mulled it over, I realized it was a good one.

Kathi and I still sit on the floor and talk. There's something wonderful about floor-sitting—people are eye to eye, close enough to touch, and it's easier to keep focused. Often when I'm talking to family or friends on the telephone, I actually sit on the floor.

In my high school office, I'm behind a desk. But when a student comes to talk, in my mind, I'm on the floor. The same thing is true when I counsel patients in my private practice.

One parent said her son begins to talk when they're alone in the car. "Sometimes," she said, "I drive all over the neighborhood until he's finished."

A couple told me they take their teens out to dinner one evening a week—to listen. One week the dad takes the son, and the mother takes the daughter. The next time they switch.

Tune in to your children and find a physical setting in which they will be willing to talk. Then listen.

Tell Me . . .

Questions! Questions! Questions! Our society tells us to ask lots of them. Even classic journalism suggests the reporter find out: who, what, where, when, why, and how. "Ask questions," the experts say, "and you've got yourself a story."

In my first master's program (counseling), the beginning edict was, "No questions. Don't ask *any* questions in therapy."

Come on, I thought. *No questions? That's how I live. I ask bunches of questions, and the stuff I find out is unbelievable. There's no way I can refrain.*

But I learned. Actually, it was drummed into me.

Funny thing about questions. We can feel as if we're being interrogated like a witness on the stand.

"How much did you pay for that?" is a question people often ask us. We might prefer to keep the information private, but we find ourselves stammering out the price. Afterward we berate ourselves for falling into the trap. We feel manipulated. It's somewhat like a fish taking bait, being jerked around by a fisherman, and flopping furiously to its untimely death.

Questioning puts the questioner in control. The person who is expected to respond is at the mercy of the questioner (like it or not).

Sally's eyes were blazing and her auburn hair flying as she bounded into my office and slammed herself into the chair opposite me.

Bet she's got a discipline referral, I thought. *God knows she's had plenty of them.*

Looking at her discipline record, I was tempted to say, "Well, Sally, what did you do this time?"

Fortunately I refrained.

"Tell me what happened in Mr. Barnett's class," I said.

Tears began to well in her dark eyes. "I just hate that man! I raised my hand to ask a question, and he said, 'What? No cookie in your mouth?' He just told the whole class how fat I am. I want to drop his class."

Sally felt humiliated and embarrassed in front of the entire class. She knew she was overweight, and it was a sore spot. She was deeply hurt.

Because I began with "Tell me" and was willing to listen, she was able to express her feelings. If I had jumped the gun and asked questions about her unacceptable behavior in class, I never would have known the underlying pain.

Now, look at a parent/teen scenario:

Pam sheepishly sneaks in the front door.

Mom:	"Hey, didn't I tell you to be home from school half an hour ago? Where were you? What were you doing? Were you with that no-good kid again? You get in here and get started on these dishes. Just wait 'til your dad gets home."
Pam:	"Get outta my face."

The fight is on!

Notice all the questions? Also, the parent doesn't seem to wait for an answer. Mom's mad. She wants to be in control but fears she's not.

Let's turn this around by using a simple phrase: "Tell me."

"Tell me" is the opposite of questioning. It allows the person who is asked to be in control of how much or how little he or she will answer.

Pam sheepishly sneaks in the front door. Mom takes a second look. She notices dirt on Pam's blouse, a rip in her jeans, and a smudge across her face. Pam looks scared.

Mom: "Pam, it looks like something is wrong. *Tell me* what happened."

Pam: (Sobbing.) "It was awful. At lunch some girls said I looked at them wrong. They ganged up on me and told me they would fight me after school. I was so scared, I ran all the way home. I kept hiding behind bushes and fell down."

As parents, we get a lot more out of our teens when we take a minute to observe their body language, respond to it, and ask them to tell us what happened.

Sometimes a teen does not want to give information.

Pam sheepishly sneaks in the front door . . . etc.

Mom: "Pam, it looks like something is wrong. *Tell me* what happened."

Pam: "Nothin', Mom."

Mom: "Okay, sweetie, but I am willing to listen if you want to talk." (Mom gives her a hug.)

Mom respected Pam's desire to be private. My guess is that at a later time Pam will be willing to tell her mother what was wrong.

"Tell me" seems like a simple formula. It is, but it works wonders. I'd encourage you to practice it—with everyone.

The "I" Message

"You make me so mad!" . . . "You always!" . . . "You never!" . . . "You should!"

Them's fightin' words. We get our defensive dukes up, and as soon as our attacker breathes, we jump in headlong defending ourselves to the max. We plain don't like it. We feel accused.

We really hadn't even listened to what the person said because we were busy preparing our retort. Maybe he or she had something valuable to say—something we needed to hear.

However, we only heard the *you*. So we got ready to counter.

Parent: "*You*'re late again! *You* make me so mad. *You*'d think I could trust *you* to call—but no, *you*'re too busy with those stupid friends of yours. *You*'re grounded—forever!"

Teen: "So?"

"You" messages put both parent and teen on the defensive. Nothing is settled.

Let's try using an "I" message instead:

Parent: "Tell me why you were late."

Teen: "No reason; we were just hangin' around."

Parent: "Craig, we have an agreement. *I* asked you to call if there was some reason you weren't able to be home on time. *I* worry when *I* don't hear from you. *I* cannot allow you to do this. *I* am grounding you for next Saturday night."

Teen: "Okay, okay."

The "I" statements hit the issue. Craig was late, there was a previous agreement ignored, and discipline was in order. Even though Craig probably wouldn't admit it, he knew his parent was being fair.

Here's another example:

Parent: "*Your* room is a pigsty. *You*'re permeating the whole house with the stench. It smells like a locker room. *You*'re filthy. It's disgusting. *You* get in here and get this place cleaned up—and I mean from top to bottom—or *you*'ll never see daylight again."

Teen: "Pick, pick, pick! That's all you ever do. Get off my back!"

When this type of communication is going on, camaraderie is out the door. There's no way the parent and teen can get on common ground.

Blaming usually brings all kinds of statements from parents that they will not be able to back up. They're rash. The kid knows it and does what he or she pleases—making matters worse.

With chagrin, I remember an episode when my daughter was six years old:

Kathi usually had a lot of stuff on her bed—clothes, games, drawings, crayons. It was getting to the point she could hardly get in her bed at night for all the junk.

Keeping a house superbly clean was a lot more important to me then than it is now. Thank goodness.

Barging into her room, I announced: "You'd better have this bed cleaned up by tomorrow afternoon at 3:00, or everything is going in the trash."

Surprise, surprise. A lot of things were still on her bed by the next day at 3:00.

Now, what do I do? I thought. *I've backed myself into a corner this time. As rash as this is, I'd better keep my word,* I reasoned.

"Kathi, I asked you to put away the things on your bed by 3:00 today. They are still there, so I must put them in the trash."

It was difficult seeing the tears seeping out the corners of her eyes, glistening on that sweet little face. But I did it.

Looking back, I wish I had put the items in a trash bag and then later allowed her to buy them back for a few cents each. The incident had a great impact on me. In future years, I was more careful not to make irrational promises in a fit of rage that would be hard to keep.

The better way is to set reasonable limits. Going back to the illustration of the adolescent's dirty room, here's a more healthy example:

Parent: "*I* hate the disorder and smell of your room. *I* would like to have you clean everything off the floor, your bed, and the dresser. *I* will expect this to be done by 5:00 P.M. Saturday. If it isn't, *I* will not allow you to go out that evening."

Teen: "Alright, alright."

There is nothing wrong with the parent making a strong statement (using the "I" message). If you notice, the parent said exactly what was expected and when. The teen could actually clean the room in about fifteen minutes, if he shoved everything in drawers and the closet (which would comply with the parent's wishes). The adolescent also was certain he would not be able to go out Saturday night if it wasn't done.

Fact versus Feeling

The windows rattled and the house seemed nearly jerked off its foundation as the door slammed. Tom's eyes were ablaze. He slam-dunked his books onto the chair. One bounced to the floor, and he kicked it with intensity.

Tom: "I hate that teacher," (he roars)—"and I got an F in math."

Dad: (His face nearly explodes, his fury matching Tom's.) "You got *what*, young man?

"If I've asked you once, I asked you a hundred times, 'Do you have any homework?' But, no. No! You never do. Well it's certainly obvious why. Who has homework when he's doing absolutely nothing in class anyway?

"Things are going to change around here. You can just forget about T.V., your CDs, the telephone, or ever getting out of this house again. It's over, buddy."

World War III has begun.

Dad did what most of us do most of the time. He responded immediately to the *factual* part of the message—the failure in math. However, he missed the *feeling* part. If we don't deal with the feeling first, we will probably have a fight on our hands. Also, we'll not be able to deal effectively with the real issue.

Our instinct is to go for the *fact*. As parents, we often jump onto our invisible soapbox and have a go at the sermon of the century.

Back to the illustration. The *feeling* message was that Tom hates the teacher. The *fact* message was the F grade. This time, see how Dad deals with the feeling first.

Tom: "I hate that teacher, and I got an F in math."

Dad: "Sounds like you had a really bad day. Tell me about it."

Tom: "Well, Mrs. Beeman gave us a problem in algebra and asked me to work it out on the board. I knew how to do it, Dad, but when I got up there, my mind went blank. My heart was pounding out of my chest, and my hands were so sweaty I could hardly hold the chalk. To make matters worse, Mrs. Beeman said, 'Well, it's obvious you haven't been doing your homework—again. No wonder you're about to fail the class. Sit down, Tom.' I was so embarrassed. The class laughed, and I was hoping the floor would open up and I could drop out of sight. I just can't face that class again."

Dad: "Tom, I'm really sorry about your embarrassment. I know algebra is a struggle for you. I'll get an appointment with Mrs. Beeman, and the three of us will work it out."

Very different outcome.

In the first example, Dad would never learn of Tom's humiliation and anxiety in class. In turn, Tom would begin to close up even more with his father, because he felt nonacceptance. Probably the F grade wouldn't improve.

In the last scene, Dad really hooked into Tom's emotional dilemma. And did you notice how much Tom told his dad? He really got it all out.

By Dad's response, Tom knew they were on the same team. He had a father who really cared about his life and was willing to go to bat for him.

If there is an explosive sentence, it usually contains a fact and a feeling. Dealing with the feeling first calms everyone down. We are then more equipped to tackle the fact logically.

Body Language

Richard cautiously slid around the door of my office and melted into the chair. His head was bent; his shoulders drooped. When he finally lifted his head, his eyes were filled with sadness. Richard sighed. It was obvious he was very troubled.

A few hours later, Sarah barged in. Eyes were ablaze, hair flying, and body taut as she sat rigidly in the chair. *Something's got her going*, I thought.

We read body language all the time. We sense the people who want to be hugged, and we get a strong feeling from those who prefer a handshake. We recognize fury, pain, frustration, and disappointment. It doesn't take a college degree to tell a lot about a person by looking at the response of his or her body.

It was a shocker the first day I walked into the dorm of the male teen prison. A six-foot-two-inch dude with bulging muscles approached me. "What are you doing here?" he blurted.

"Nothing," I felt like saying. Good sense was telling me to run for the door and never come back.

"I'm here to counsel anyone who's interested," I cautiously replied.

The young prisoners began gathering around to see a petite Norwegian blond, who looked about as out of place as a bull in a china shop.

"You gettin' paid for this?" one asked.

"Nope," I answered.

"Doing this because you're in school or something?" another volunteered.

"No," I responded.

"So what's in it for you?" one glared.

"Nothing," I retorted.

With his hands in his pockets, one teen looked up and asked, "What kind of stuff can we talk about?"

I breathed a sigh of relief. "Anything you want." Then, looking over the emerging group, I wisely added, "Except sex."

"Can I be first?" one asked. Another kid shoved him and said, "Hey, man, you can be second."

The first day was so exhilarating, I continued twice a week for three years.

Those adolescents were men! I didn't treat them as ordinary sixteen- or eighteen-year-olds. Most had run the streets since they were nine. They were in for robbery, drug dealing, rape, and murder. One fellow had been charged with fifteen murders.

Needless to say, I learned much about the criminal mind and the streets.

Survival taught me to read their body language. I couldn't count on what they said—they lied. All the time.

Our mouths may lie, but our bodies tell the truth. So, if the body movements don't match what the mouth is saying—beware. Sometimes when I've detected a lie because the body and statements didn't mesh, I've pointed it out.

"I'm confused. Your body is telling me something very different than what you're saying," I've commented to the prison inmates. Thinking I could read their minds, they have looked at me with wide eyes and blurted out the truth. If only they knew.

So pay attention to what the body is saying, as well as to the words.

Healing Notes

As a therapist, I've seen miracles happen when patients write honest, caring, confrontive letters. Communication comes out differently in writing.

First, we are able to carefully think through what we need to say. It can be rewritten until it says exactly what we mean. Instead of sending "You" messages ("you made me so mad"), use "I" statements. ("I need to talk with you about something that really bothered me. I'm angry.")

Face-to-face confrontation can make it difficult to be honest in a kind, tactful way. And the person to whom we're talking is generally waiting until we breathe so he or she can defend himself or herself.

On the contrary, when the person receives our letter, he or she can read it with a more open heart. Each time the note is read, the person is usually more responsive.

Dolores brought her teenage son into counseling because of her impending divorce. The son only had a few sessions, but Dolores stayed.

There were a number of childhood issues we dealt with, as well as the divorce. I knew there was a great problem between Dolores and her father. She felt unloved, disrespected, and abandoned, and she could hardly stand the thought of him. Her parents were divorced when she was an adolescent.

"Going to send a Father's Day card to your dad?" I ventured in one session. Boy, that lit a fire!

Continuing, I gingerly asked, "How do you connect the biblical injunction, 'honor your father and mother,' with your feelings for your dad?"

Months later, after many hours of recounting and reliving the pain of her childhood, Dolores had come to grips with her feelings and the need to eventually forgive her father. She wrote and rewrote an honest letter. Sliding it in the mailbox brought mixed feelings of relief and anxiety. Would he answer?

"If he answers this letter," Dolores said, "it will be his typical response—blaming me, my mom, everyone. He'll never admit to having had any part in my pain."

Two weeks later my answering service said, "There's an emergency call from Dolores."

Almost breathlessly, Dolores answered my call back with, "Bob (she can't call him Dad) answered my letter. I just can't bring myself to open it, so I'll wait until my appointment with you."

Dropping onto the sofa in my office several days later, Dolores told me, "I couldn't stand it until I got in here, so I read the letter just now in the waiting room."

Tears welled in my own eyes as she read aloud the letter from her father. He empathized, expressed love, took responsibility for what he had done, and asked forgiveness. He told of his own journey with his parents—the estrangement, which ended a few years prior to their deaths, and his struggle to forgive them.

Even though this was a healing event, there are still issues with which Dolores struggles in relation to her father. But her giant leap propelled her on the road toward forgiveness.

Often I have asked parents and teens to write detailed letters to each other about issues on which they clash. More often than not, it brings about understanding and restoration.

Then there are simple, everyday notes. Some are funny, cute, ridiculous, sweet—whatever the mood. Written messages have a way of touching.

Notes can be put on the fridge (the first place a teen heads after entering the house). On a rare occasion, consider making your child's bed and pin a note to the pillow. Stick one in his or her schoolbook, notebook, lunch, on the car windshield (if your teen drives), etc. Let your imagination take off.

"Roses are red, violets are blue" is a simple way to begin a poem. Others can just say, "I love you. Have a good day." Or, "I heard a nice compliment about you" (then repeat it). Another note can state, "I'm proud of you because . . ."

Be creative. The more you practice, the better you'll become at effectively and uniquely sending a message of love.

When I counsel teens at school, I write them a note. To other students, I pass on compliments I've overheard. Sometimes I just tell them what nice people they are. Other times it's a note to encourage them. "I'm proud of you," I often write. My notes are handwritten, because I want students to know they are from me—not something I asked my secretary to do.

Kids almost always drop by to thank me. Often I've seen tears of appreciation—even in the guys. One parent told me her son framed my letter.

Whenever we get a kind note from someone, it makes our day. So take a moment of your time to be emotionally connected with your adolescent through a written word of encouragement. It will bring the closeness you desire, eventually.

Touching

Sparky is a little, pure white, fluffy Highland terrier. She was about nine months old when I got her. As I snapped her leash onto her collar for our very first walk, her little body was quivering with excitement and her eyes seemed to be dancing. I cuddled her face in my hands and said, "You're so sparky!" *That's it,* I thought, *I'll name her Sparky.*

Now Sparky loves to be touched. When I get home, she's jumping on the outside of the sliding glass door, wanting to be noticed (as though I could ignore her). She wants her tummy rubbed, her hindquarters massaged, and her ears scratched. And she won't give up until we have a lot of touching "conversation."

Humans need to be touched too. At times, I've wished I could be as aggressive as Sparky—really let the person know I want to be touched.

Children do it. They're all over us when they need affection. Tragically, it all begins to change around puberty. They stand off. The need for touch is so enormous, yet teens pretend they could not care less.

Kim nearly knocked me over as she flew into my arms and said, "I just came for my hug." She was a delightful, needy girl. For months, she came in several times a day for a hug.

"I can't stand my mom touching me," Kim once declared. "She makes me sick." They had knock-down-drag-out battles almost daily, with four-letter words flying around the room. Respect was virtually gone, and love was not far behind.

But Kim still needed love. Fortunately, she came to me to get it in a healthy way. My goal was to teach the mother and daughter how to handle their issues so they could have a good relationship. It eventually worked for them.

One patient in my private practice said, "Jeenie, you know what impressed me the most about our first session?" (I was expecting some deep psychological breakthrough.) "You hugged me when I left," she continued. "You'll never know how much I needed it."

Often adolescents are able to take advice, honesty, and physical touch from an outsider much easier than from their parents. The basic reason is they are trying to separate from their parents and become more adult. Even though their need to individuate is strong, so is their need for a loving touch.

I encourage parents to physically touch their teenager. The touching will need to change a bit, though, because teens are often embarrassed and unable to welcome the same kind of expression of love they received as children. However, playful touches are acceptable to adolescents—a gentle jab on the shoulder, frisky tickle, fun-loving tap on the nose, tender squeeze of the hand, comforting pat on the shoulder, brisk neck and back rub, an occasional hug, and maybe even a quick kiss.

If your teen is into hugs and kisses, though—go for it!

Teen Bedtime Routine

It may seem a bit strange to tuck an adult-sized adolescent into bed. However, it can be a time when love is given by the parent and more easily accepted by the teenager.

When your offspring is in bed, knock at the door and ask, "May I come in?" While gently tucking in the covers, say a few appreciative words (i.e., "I'm so proud of you because . . ." or "I appreciate the way you . . ."). Say a short prayer, thanking God for your child and asking for a good night's rest. Top it off with a light kiss on the forehead.

It does wonders.

"I Love You"

Tracie was one of the prettiest girls I've met. Her body was like that of a model, and her face was delicate and beautiful.

We talked often, always ending with a hug. She was warm, honest, tender, and needy.

Home wasn't all that great for Tracie. When bitter fights ensued, Tracie held her own. She could cuss like a drunken sailor.

One day when Tracie plopped into the chair across from me, I noticed signs of abuse. She recounted she had been pulled around the room by her hair, slammed into furniture, and choked.

Legally, I had to submit a suspected child abuse report. Parents were contacted by the authorities, and steps were taken to help the family cope in healthy ways.

Months later Tracie came back to see me. Tears welled in her vivid blue eyes and trickled down her face as she said, "Last night, my mom said, 'I love you.'"

Teens do need to hear those words from us—regardless of what we've been through as parents or how beastly they have behaved toward us.

Say it—often! Honest, caring communication is the foundation of healthy relationships. Give it a whirl.

Coming to Grips

1. "Hey, kid, you make me so mad. You're late again!" Change this sentence to an "I" message.
   "I ____________________________________."

2. "That school stinks, and I'm flunking out."
   Respond to the *feeling* first. ____________________
   Respond to the *fact*. __________________________
   ____

3. Write down five ways to physically touch your child:
   a. ______________________________________
   b. ______________________________________
   c. ______________________________________
   d. ______________________________________
   e. ______________________________________

4. Listen to your teen for five minutes. Let nothing interrupt. Maybe start by saying, "Tell me all about your day." If he or she doesn't respond, say, "Tell me something funny (or sad) that happened." Or, "Tell me what a teacher did," etc. Try sitting on the floor.

5. Write out three notes and put them in special places for your adolescent.

2

Corralling Those Suckers

W*hat big, brown, sad eyes*, I thought, looking into the face of Troy. He cradled his face in his hands as his body slumped in the chair.

"Know something?" he slowly began. "My parents don't give a hang about me. Hey, they couldn't care less where I am, what guys I'm with, when I come in—or if I do. Doesn't matter to them. If they loved me, they'd give me some limits—some rules."

Brad was different. He had an air of confidence, went to class, did his homework, got decent grades. "I have a curfew, and I'd better be there or call," he volunteered. "My parents know where I'm going and who I'm with. They keep pretty good track of me because they love me."

Okay, Jeenie, you're probably thinking, *so you've heard kids say this a time or two*. Surprise, surprise. I've heard this constantly from thousands of teens for nearly twenty years.

However, if you think your kids will say it to you—you're dead wrong. That's just not what kids do. They scream and yell, threaten, and tell you, "I'm the only kid in the whole school who has limits of any kind."

But when the chips are down and they're alone with me in my office, they admit the truth—"I *need* my parents to set limits. It helps me know I'm loved."

Holding the Reins

Remember when your child was little and Christmas came along with a brand-new red bicycle draped in holiday ribbon? "I want to ride my bike," your kid screamed, forgetting all else.

You put your child on the bike. Then you desperately tried to hold on and not topple the swaying two-wheeler as he or she bounced up and down with excitement. After a few instructions on how to pedal, steer, and brake, the first ride began. Your child wobbled back and forth as you held the seat and ran alongside. In a few years, he or she was careening all over the neighborhood.

Your child probably could have learned to ride that bicycle without help, but it would have meant lots more bruises, bloody knees, torn jeans, and fear. By holding the seat steady (putting limits on him or her), the learning process went a lot easier—for both of you.

So it is with teens. Adolescents desperately *need* and *want* limits—a relatively tight rein. It gives them a feeling of security. In these days of accelerated peer pressure, teens may need an "out"—to be able to say, "My parents won't let me do that." Then they and their friends can commiserate about how awful their parents are (and they will). Yet, they still feel accepted by their group.

When my daughter was an adolescent, she asked permission to go to an event. It was okay with me, but as I looked at her face, her body language was saying something else. "Kathi, do you need for me to say 'No'?" I asked. Rather sheepishly she grinned and with a sigh of relief answered, "Yeah."

Standing up to friends is very difficult for teens—it's hard enough as adults. Being different and not going along with the crowd can be uncomfortable. Therefore, adolescents need the security and support of a parent who will set limits and stick with them.

Building the Corral

Horses run free within the corral. They enjoy lots of latitude within the safe confines of the fences.

As parents, though, we sometimes forget to allow our teens the freedom they need within the safe boundaries. We often get into the habit of saying a quick "No."

When our teen begins with, "Mom, could I . . . ," out of our mouth shoots a resounding "No!" Much of the time we haven't waited to hear the full request. It's just easier to say "No." We don't have to drive them anywhere, pick them up, collaborate with other parents, juggle our schedule, be inconvenienced.

My suggestion is just the opposite. Be ready to say "Yes." Most of the requests are rather trivial and do not matter all that much. Give your teen the view that most of his or her requests can be accommodated, especially if he or she gives you time to think it through and/or work out a compromise.

Then, when the big "No" comes, it will have a greater impact, and often the teen is more willing to accept your decision.

So give your fillies lots of room within their corral.

The Corral Blueprint

The key in building a corral (setting limits) is allowing your teenager to experience the *logical consequences* of his or her behavior.

My twelve-year-old Chevy and I took our last ride together—to the new car dealer. After spending multiple thousands of dollars on my pile of junk, I decided enough was enough. With vigor I slammed the door, rattling the windows—glad to be walking away from the mess.

Sliding into the seat of my brand-new, red car was wonderful. It even had an air conditioner that worked and a stereo/cassette unit that caressed the interior of the automobile with music. It sounded like Surround Sound. My old car had an AM radio that I had to keep slapping.

Slamming into first gear, I roared onto the freeway. By third gear, I realized this baby could move. By fourth, I was having a hard time holding those horses down.

Speed has always excited me. At one point in my life, I dreamed of being a race-car driver. Shifting gears has always been a power thing for me. There's a sense of being in control of a mighty engine.

For sake of illustration, let's pretend I revved it up to 120 miles per hour. It would be euphoric—the feel of the engine surging, the excitement of the ride sending adrenaline coursing through my veins. If I went far enough (unharmed), I would eventually see some red, blinking lights behind me.

"Ma'am, could I see your driver's license and registration, please?" the officer would ask.

"Sure," I respond, fumbling in my purse and glove compartment.

"Know how fast you were going? I clocked you at 120 miles per hour. You're lucky we didn't have to scoop you off the pavement with a spoon," he continues. "Maybe this ticket will be a little reminder."

"About how much will it cost?" I venture.

"Two hundred dollars," he answers.

As I drive away I keep thinking, *Two hundred bucks! That's a bundle. Wow, two hundred smackers.*

Because I chose to not discipline myself, I had to pay the *logical consequences* for my actions.

Conversely, let's say I made a decision to drive the speed limit—boring. I could save the money and buy something I really wanted. (For those of you wondering, most of the time I'm within the speed limits.)

Our teenagers need to feel the logical consequences of their actions.

Ron was a fun-loving kid. He laughed a lot, got himself in predicaments, had a good time, and got lots of attention (some good, some bad).

His math teacher, Mr. Stone, had enough of this kid and sent him to my office on a discipline referral—again. Mr. Stone also had the misfortune to have Ron in his science class.

Now Ron was definitely not a college prep student. He took math and science because it was required to graduate. As long as he squeaked through, that's all he wanted. Learning something would only be a by-product.

"Hi," he grinned, as he meekly tiptoed into my office. Slipping quietly into the chair, he waited for the guillotine to drop.

"Hi, Ron. Tell me what happened in Mr. Stone's room," I said.

With head down, he softly said, "Well, I sorta spit."

"Spit?" I quizzed.

"Uh-huh," he returned.

Reading the referral, I found that Ron had taken a big gulp of water from the water fountain, then spit at students.

Looking at me from the corner of his eyes, this kid was expecting the worst.

"Tell you what, Ron," I began, "we're going to make a deal here."

His eyes brightened, then turned to puzzlement.

"Sounds like Mr. Stone is sick to death of you," I continued, "especially when he has you for two classes. Our deal is simple: Every time Mr. Stone sends you out on referral, he will just give you the paper—no comments. And there will be no lectures from me. None. You can count on it. Instead, I'll automatically give you two hours' detention. Real simple. Since you have Mr. Stone twice a day, this could add up to four hours of detention daily. Understood?"

"Yeah," Ron returned.

"My suggestion is," I replied, "the next time you decide you want to spit water, do it in a big way. Get your mouth as full as you possibly can, then let it rip—get every single person in the class really good, because you have two hours' detention. However, you also have the choice to swallow the water and save yourself the consequences. It's up to you."

I never saw Ron again on referral the rest of high school.

Several years after graduation, he popped around my door. "Remember me?"

"Ron, how nice to see you!" I exclaimed. "Tell me what's happening in your life."

"I got myself a really good job. I'm laying brick. I keep getting raises, and they've asked me if I would like to become a partner in the company. So I'm saving my money, and it looks like I'll be able to do it in about a year," he announced.

Ron had learned about making good choices and reaping positive consequences.

In setting parameters, as parents we need to (1) tell them *exactly* what is expected, and (2) spell out the consequences of disobedience.

Here's a rather typical exchange between parent and teen:

Dad: "The car is filthy. Get it washed."
Teen: (with eyes glued on a video he mutters) "Okay, okay."

The next day . . .

Dad: "Hey, didn't I tell you to get that car washed? Listen, when I talk, you move. Do you hear me?"
Teen: "But, Dad . . ."
Dad: "Don't you 'but' me. You just do as I say and ask questions later."

In this scene, Dad wasn't *specific* about what he wanted or what would happen if it wasn't done.

Let's try a different approach:

Dad: "Son."
Teen: "Huh?" (still glued to the video).
Dad: "I want you to stop the video for a minute."
Teen: (video stops) "What?"
Dad: "I want you to wash the car. You have until 6:00 P.M. tomorrow. If you haven't washed it, you will not be allowed to drive this weekend. Is that clear?"
Teen: "Yeah."

Six-thirty Saturday night, the teenager barges into the house and slides into Dad.

Teen: "Hey, Dad. I need the keys. The guys are waiting."

Dad: "Son, we had an agreement. You did not live up to it. The car was not washed by 6:00 P.M."

Teen: "Dad, come on. Don't do this. I promised my buddies a week ago I'd drive. Give me the keys."

Dad: "Sorry, son. You did not live up to our agreement."

Adolescents also deserve the right to know what is expected of them and what consequences will ensue. They then have to decide if the consequences are worth it. Often teens don't believe negative repercussions will follow. So they go for it. When they do, the parents need to be ready.

"Whoa, Boy!"

Picture a ball game between the two of us. You throw the ball; I catch it and return it. The next time you toss it to me, I let it drop. Suppose you pick it up and whirl it, but I again make no attempt to catch it. The ball game is over. Even if you angrily send the ball smashing into my face, as long as I do not respond, there's no game. It's finished.

So often we get into a ball game of tossing words back and forth—defending ourselves.

Parent: "Hey, didn't I tell you to pick up your room?"

Teen: "That's not fair; you just want a slave around here."

Parent: "Excuse me! You never lift a finger to do anything around here. I work hard all day and just ask one little thing from you.

But, no. You can't be bothered. You make me sick."

Teen: "Well, if you think I'm ever gonna clean my room again, you're crazy."

Parent: "Crazy? You just shut your mouth."

Teen: "Hey, I'll say whatever I want!"

Parent: "Did you hear me? I said shut up!"

Teen: "Get outta my face!"

The parent and teenager are having a verbal ball game—throwing the garbage back and forth. It never turns out productive.

Let's change the scene. The parent refuses to get into an oral exchange. Instead, he uses the word *regardless* or *nevertheless* with a short phrase, which brings them back to the root of the problem—the teen chose not to obey.

Parent: "I asked you to pick your clothes off the floor and bed and either hang them up or put them in the hamper. I also asked you to clean off the papers on your dresser and chest of drawers and either throw them out, place them in your notebook, or stack them neatly. This was to be done by 7:00 P.M. today or T.V. would be off limits for the rest of the week. I see it's not done. Therefore, there will be no T.V."

Teen: "That's not fair! You just want a slave around here."

Parent: "*Regardless*, you did not live up to our agreement."

Teen: "You make me so mad. No one else does this to their kid."

Parent: "*Regardless*, you did not live up to our agreement."

Teen: "Well, if you think I'm ever gonna clean my room again, you're crazy."

Parent: "*Nevertheless*, you did not live up to our agreement."

By this time, the adolescent will get the message. The parent stopped the ball game by choosing not to defend himself. No matter what the teen said, the parent stuck to one small phrase and never veered.

For practice, try this with a friend. Then switch roles. You can feel the futility of trying to manipulate other people when they constantly come back with *regardless* or *nevertheless* and a short phrase. You finally give up, realizing they can't be broken down.

Kids tend to harangue and harass a parent because getting their own selfish way is of utmost importance. So they keep it up. They know parents tend to give in to pressure. The stress is too much and, at times, all parents throw up their hands in defeat. "I don't care; just do what you want," a weary parent laments. But since we're in parenting for the long haul, using the word *regardless* or *nevertheless* connected to a phrase gives us the fortitude to continue.

Sam came into my private office for his therapy session. He had a funny, little grin on his face, which merged into an abbreviated chuckle as he sank into the sofa.

"Okay, Sam, why the laugh?" I asked.

"I did your *regardless/nevertheless* trick—and it worked!" he replied.

"Tell me what happened," I returned.

"Remember how my wife was bugging me to take the long weekend and visit her folks upstate?" he continued.

"Yes."

"Well she nagged me for days," said Sam. "Finally I said, 'Look, Linda, I just don't feel comfortable with your parents.

Your mom and you are off with the kids, and as soon as I try to strike up a conversation with your dad, he heads for the garage to work on the car. I've even gone outside and offered to help, but he just grunts. So I stand around for hours in the grease trying to make small talk. No response. They didn't want you to marry me, and no matter what I do, it just doesn't work. I'm not willing to spend three days in misery. Why don't you and the kids go. I know they really want to see you, and I have no problem with your going.'

"From then on, Linda really put on the pressure. So I decided to try that *nevertheless* thing you told me about. I figured out a phrase and had it ready.

"The next time Linda brought it up, I said, 'I'm uncomfortable around your folks, and I choose not to go.' Every time she countered, I began with *nevertheless* and repeated my sentence.

"After three days, she looked at me and said, 'You really aren't going, are you?'

"She took the kids and had a wonderful weekend. So did I."

Coming to Grips

1. Complete this sentence. As the parent of a teenager, most of the time I:
   a. set logical limits and stick to them
   b. give limits but eventually yield to the pressure
   c. am rather lax and inconsistent with limits

2. What is your usual reason for giving in to pressure from your teenager? ______________________________

   ____

   ____

   ____

3. If you are lax, what is keeping you from limiting your adolescent? Are you afraid? ______________________

4. Write out specific instructions as to what you want from your teen. ______________________

Now, include the consequences of disobedience. ______

5. Think back on an episode in which your teen badgered you. Use the word *regardless* or *nevertheless*, then come up with an appropriate phrase.

3

The Art of Making Your Adolescent Mind (without Losing Yours)

> It is the tasks connected with the home that are the fundamental tasks of humanity. . . . If the mother does not do her duty, there will either be no next generation, or a next generation that is worse than none at all.
>
> Theodore Roosevelt

How insightful. Doing our duty isn't easy. It's gut-level hard work, thankless, and often discouraging.

The good news is when parents are fairly consistent as disciplinarians, adolescents turn out well. Sometimes they're twenty years old before the training seems to take hold—but it does. Eventually.

Punishment versus Discipline

Punishment gets even. It pays that sucker back—gives him what he deserves. And it's easy. Like second nature.

Conversely, discipline is fair. It fits the crime. Discipline takes all the details into account, then metes out justice.

Kelly was a wild one. She screamed at teachers and shouted obscenities—a whirlwind of fire and brimstone.

What was that noise? I thought. I heard yelling, and the building seemed to vibrate. Then the noise increased. Kelly had flung open the door to the attendance office and crashed it into the wall. As though that were not enough, she then violently grabbed the door and slammed it shut, rattling almost every window in the building, while all the time screaming obscenities at the top of her lungs.

Moments later, the attendance clerk hauled Kelly into my office.

"This kid came to school barefoot, and it's winter," she said. "Do something."

"Tell me what's going on, Kelly," I asked.

Tears began to well up. "My mom and me had this huge fight. I'm going for a job interview after school, so I wore a dress and wanted to wear hose and heels. Before I could finish dressing, we had the blowout, so I just left."

Picking up the telephone, I called Kelly's mom to ask her to bring hose and shoes. "Let me talk to that kid," Mom responded.

Before Mom could begin, Kelly used some of the most vile language I've heard. She called her mom everything in the book—and more.

Kelly handed the phone back to me.

"I am shocked, Kelly," I announced. "Your language and disrespect to your mother are appalling. I'm disgusted. You are *never* to use such crude language around me again. Furthermore, the screaming and door slamming are also off limits. Is that understood? Now, please step outside my office while I speak with your mother."

"Okay," she meekly replied. "I'm really sorry, Mrs. Gordon."

"Have you ever heard anything worse, Mrs. Gordon?" whispered her mother. "I've done everything in the world for Kelly, and this is what I get. We've allowed her to have whatever she wanted and have never disciplined her. What do I do now?"

"Well, Mrs. Reid," I responded, "the correction should have begun at age two. It's too late now. All you can do is wait until she's eighteen and make her move out."

Undisciplined children grow into out-of-control teenagers. They also feel unloved and are unstable.

One of the first steps in being a good disciplinarian is to logically think about the action. A lot of behavior will be just dumb kid things—the kind of stuff most of us did. Ask the question, "How bad is it?" On a scale of one to ten, where would it fall?

Second, take a good look at what kind of person your teen is. What are his or her good qualities?

Often we call together the counselor, teachers, and school psychologist for a meeting with the parents and student to see how we can help an adolescent who is in deep trouble.

We begin by listing positive attributes of the teenager. I've watched the face of the young person. Often he or she seems surprised that people have good things to say. So much of what he or she has heard has been negative.

Discipline demands creativity and consistency. So calm down, and decide what you can do to produce lasting change.

Separate the Act from the Person

Her dark brown eyes glistened with tears. I've seen that look scores of times.

"Are you busy?" she asked.

"Of course not, Maria," I answered. "Come on in."

She's pregnant, I thought.

"It doesn't seem like things are going well for you," I ventured.

Through an explosion of tears, Maria sobbed the words, "I'm going to have a baby." Her body shook with the overwhelming presence of pain and terror.

"We just did it once. Honest!" she cried. "My parents won't understand. They will throw me out."

They did.

I found a home for Maria, and she chose to place the baby for adoption.

I'm sure the parents were shocked and in enormous pain when they learned of the pregnancy. Understandable. They were unable, however, to separate the one-time act of intercourse from Maria—the person. It was all meshed together. To them, a wrong action meant their daughter was a terrible person.

Everyone does bad things—even good people. Yet too often we conclude that if someone exhibits faulty behavior, that person is totally bad. David was called "a man after God's heart" (quite an honor bestowed by Jehovah), yet he had blatantly committed adultery and was a murderer. God separated out the horrid, sinful action from the personhood of King David, thereby giving him the option to repent, be sorrowful, and turn his life around.

In my office, I've framed an anonymous quotation that captures my belief about teens.

Everyone is a potential winner.
Some people are disguised as losers.
Don't let their appearances fool you!

Concentrate on the Biggies

We parents too often let the trivial actions and fads become humongous battles. When a great deal of energy is expended on the inconsequential areas of our teen's life, it robs us of the vitality to be consistent, solid, and unbending in the areas of major importance. It is better to save our strength for when we must say "No" and make it stick.

Clean rooms often loom large with parents. I'm convinced children need to be taught personal cleanliness, how to pick up their room, and how to live in an orderly fashion. This training has great value. However, the key word is *children*.

Teens are no longer children. Granted they often act as though they are, but categorically they are not.

Even though I think a clean room is ideal, it's not much of a reality for most adolescents. In the mid to late teens, most kids have rooms that look as though a tornado has swooped down and swirled everything around a couple of times. Sometimes it even smells bad.

I vividly recall my fellow male collegians bragging about the fact they had not changed their sheets all year. Yuk! Now, well into adulthood, there is not a dirty one in the bunch. They're esteemed professional men, who would be embarrassed if it were known how they lived in college.

There isn't any kid I know of who died of a dirty room. If it becomes too much of a hassle, my suggestion is to say:

"I'm tired of asking you to clean up your room. I've decided you can live in filth if you choose. However, I just about get nauseous when I pass your room. I'd like my food to stay down, so would you please keep your door closed. I don't appreciate the smell permeating the rest of our home. Thanks."

For those of you who can't go along with a disorderly room, refer back to the previous chapter for illustrations of how to accomplish the goal—setting the parameters while making the teen aware of the logical consequences.

Cee Cee was an out-of-control person. The worse she felt, the more desperate she was to control everyone and everything around her. She constantly dragged her three kids into therapy so I could "fix 'em." What little we accomplished in the counseling sessions went out the door with them. Mama screamed, pushed, and shoved the kids down the hall as I limply looked on. Even confrontational therapy with Cee Cee seemed to do no good. She was bent on changing everyone but herself. *They* were the problem.

Yanking her twelve-year-old daughter into my office one day, she began to screech before I could get the door closed.

"Know what this dumb kid did?" she yelled.

I didn't bother to answer. It was like talking to running water.

"She shaved her legs without my permission!" Cee Cee exploded.

I was less than horrified.

After minutes of a continuing tirade, she simmered down and said, "It doesn't seem like you think it's all that big of a deal, Jeenie."

"Well, Cee Cee, most girls eventually shave their legs," I responded. "You're right that I don't think it's that traumatic. I think you should save all this uproar for the biggies."

Her eyes blazed as she retorted, "Like what?"

"Like when your son shaves his legs," I answered.

It's important to keep things in perspective. Concentrate on the big things. Don't sweat the small stuff.

Negotiation

Nobody is all that interested in giving in—even a little. We want what we want. Our way is right, and we deserve to get our request. For most of us, selfishness will not be conquered to any great extent.

Bartering is my bag. I get excited when I can bargain. One of my favorite things is the Jewelry Mart. It's a store with many counters—each is privately owned. Every month I save a small amount of money, and in about a year or so, I head for the shop.

On one such trip, I began looking for a certain kind of bracelet. Going from counter to counter, I collected prices and dickered a little. When I had narrowed it down to two shops, negotiating began in earnest. Each proprietor gave me his "very best price." The pressure was on. Each suggested I put it on layaway or put a little cash down. "No thank you; I need to think this over." Then I left.

In a day or so I went back, ogled the beautiful bracelets, and decided with which shopkeeper I wanted to deal. Digging into my purse, I brought out his business card on which I'd written the last price. "I would really like to purchase the bracelet, but I am not willing to pay $———. I'll give you half."

"Oh, no. No," the owner responded. His brow was furrowed, and his fingers tapped furiously on the hand calculator. Turning the calculator toward me, he showed his lowest price. It was getting better.

I'll see if I can get him down 20 percent, I thought. As I quoted the new price, he shook his head and pretended he was taking a huge cut.

"I will pay cash," I said.

"Okay," he agreed and lowered the price another 5 percent.

I took the bills out of my wallet, fanned them out on the counter, and counted them aloud. Then I added, "This includes tax."

"No, no," the proprietor answered.

"Okay. Well, thank you," I returned. Slowly and deliberately, I began to scoop up the dollar bills.

Before I could get them into my purse, he said, "I'll take it."

We were both satisfied. We had completed a negotiation.

In negotiation, it is vital that each person give a little and end up feeling he or she was treated fairly. When I bargain for jewelry, my intent is not to get something for nothing or take away a person's honest profit. I want it to be fair for both of us. In fact, if it's not, the owner will not accept the deal.

In negotiation, both parties must believe they are being treated in an honest and fair manner. It is important that we:

1. Acknowledge the feelings of the person with whom we negotiate. "I understand . . ."
2. State what we want. "However, I want . . ."
3. Tell the person what we are willing to do. "I am willing to . . ."
4. Ask what the other person is willing to do. "What are you willing to do?"

Then we negotiate until both are satisfied.

Parent: "*I understand* you really hate English and can see no reason to ever learn the definition of a verb or an adjective.

"*However, I want* you to graduate, and unless you pass the class, this will not happen.

"*I am willing to* accept a C grade in the course.

"*What are you willing to do?*"

Teen: "There's no way I can pass this stupid class. I can't get no C."
Parent: "What are you willing to do?"
Teen: "Okay, I will work every day in class. If I have homework, I will work a half hour on it."
Parent: "I appreciate that. If you hold up your end of the bargain, I am willing to accept a D in English. But, I expect C's in your other courses. Agreed?"
Teen: "Yeah. Agreed."

In bargaining, there is a hierarchy. Simply put, start at a higher level than you really want so you can negotiate down. Mom decided a D in English would be acceptable, but she could not start haggling at that point. She began by requesting a C grade (higher), so she had room to negotiate. Her teen had an F grade and was willing to negotiate to a D. Both the parent and adolescent believed they were treated fairly and that the D grade was realistic and reachable.

One last word on negotiation. Negotiate only one issue at a time. It keeps the focus on the situation and, consequently, is more easily resolved.

Self-Discipline

Brandon's mom thought negotiation was stupid. She just *told* him how it would be. Constantly. Therefore, Brandon was not accustomed to making any decisions on his own. He just waited for adults to decide for him, and he meekly took whatever they dished out.

One would think Brandon would be a cooperative student, but he got in lots of trouble because he had not learned self-control. He was constantly in my office for one class disturbance after another.

"You know something, Brandon," I said one day, "it's about time you began to do some of your own discipline. Since you're the one who's been messing up in class, I want you to tell me what your discipline needs to be."

"Huh?" he responded. His blank eyes looked a bit puzzled.

"Tell me what discipline you need to have for your problem in the classroom," I returned.

"I dunno," he shrugged. "Like what?"

"Well, there's one hour detention, Saturday school, two hours detention, three-day class suspension, a call to your dad, or anything else you can think of," I suggested. "What's your pleasure?"

His eyes grew large, he sat up straight and said, "Mrs. Gordon, I can't do this. You do it. I just can't. Please, Mrs. Gordon."

"Brandon, I'm not the one who had the problem in class. You are. So, you will need to determine your own discipline," I returned.

"Uh, two hours, I guess," he replied.

"Two hours of what, Brandon?"

"Detention. Two hours of detention," he added.

Writing his decision on the referral form, I continued, "Okay, when will you do the detention?"

"How about Friday?" he continued.

Brandon had a look of relief on his face. We continued to talk about self-discipline—what it is; what it means. Seldom did I see him on discipline problems after that.

The desired end result is for our children to learn to discipline themselves. If they don't, society will—severely.

One Last Word

There are three organizations that have made great contributions in helping parents discipline their adolescents:

- The Parent Project
  2848 Longhorn Street
  Ontario, CA 91761
  1-800-372-8886
  Parenting of troubled teens
- Tough Love
  P. O. Box 70
  Sellersville, PA 18960
  1-800-333-1069
  Provides parental support groups
- Back in Control
  112 East Chapman
  Orange, CA 92666
  (714) 538-6387
  Book: *Back in Control*, Fireside & Colophon, 1992, New York, NY

Christian bookstores are also continually stocking new titles on the subject of discipline.

Discipline is good—for everyone!

Coming to Grips

1. On a scale of 1–10, where do you tend to fall?

   1 2 3 4 5 6 7 8 9 10

   punish ———————————————— discipline

2. Describe a time when you separated the act from the person. ____

3. Think of a time you meshed it all together. How could you have done it differently? ______________________
____
____
____

4. Your child wants to do something with which you disagree. Write down a negotiation.

   "I understand you want ______________________
   ____

   However, I want ______________________________
   ____

   I am willing to ______________________________
   ____

What are you willing to do?"

"But You're Still My Baby"

Rescues are a constant theme of media news coverage. Heroic efforts are employed in fires, bus accidents, avalanches, airplane crashes, fires, and floods. We are intrigued with the techniques and courageous acts of people who put their lives on the line to rescue others.

Then there are protectors. Parents. They constantly protect their young children from running into the street, playing with matches, using knives, putting dangerous things in their mouths, climbing hazardous objects, and poking things into electrical outlets. God gave parents as protectors of children.

Rescue and protection, however, are two different things.

Rescuing

In working with over eight thousand adolescents, the thing that I observe as being one of the most damaging is *parental rescuing*.

My definition of *rescuing* is allowing a teenager to cop out—encouraging him or her to believe there are no consequences to behavior. The teen thinks someone else will always fix it. How very harmful and debilitating is this practice. The adolescent is deprived of becoming self-sufficient and independent.

Anthony was a middle child. He was diagnosed as having a learning disability and spent his school years in special education classes.

He oozed with personality. Anthony was fun, enjoyed life, and freely expressed himself. A free spirit.

"Just Say No" had *not* become his motto. He was a drug user. In order to support his habit, he became involved in a variety of illegal activities.

Mom was single and panic-stricken. Dad wasn't very involved with his son.

Anthony had a pattern. He would get caught in one of his unlawful schemes, spread-eagle as he was searched and then handcuffed, take another ride to the police station, and be booked. As soon as he could get to a phone—you guessed it—he called Mom. Posthaste, Mom begged, borrowed (never stole) the bail, and tore into the city jail to rescue her little Anthony—again. Not only was it getting quite expensive, but it was taking an emotional toll on her.

Frantically she called me. "Anthony is back in jail," she cried. "This time the bail is $1,000, and I just don't know how I'm going to get the money. I have cleaned out my savings, taken salary advances, used my credit card, and borrowed from friends and family. What should I do?"

"Leave him there," I replied.

Tears nearly splashed through the phone. Terror oozed through her voice. "I just can't," she sobbed.

"Anthony has been in and out of jail so many times, I can hardly count," I explained. "I've heard this same story from you over and over, seen your tears, and witnessed the traumatic effect it has on you. It's time Anthony spends a night behind bars. He must face the consequences of his behavior. Otherwise, his chances of changing are slim."

Mom got up her courage and left him in the cell overnight.

Until Mom was willing to go to the wall, Anthony would not change. He didn't have to because Mom took care of his consequences. She always got him off the hook. Why should he change? He liked having the best of both worlds.

Anthony also had little respect for his mother. It didn't matter to him she practically had to hock her soul to continually get bail money. It never entered his mind to pay her back. He took the freedom and ran—back to his life of crime and drugs.

Once Mom decided to stop her destructive pattern, Anthony came face-to-face with a big dose of reality. He had to contend with a night in a dank, dirty, smelly jail cell among people he considered to be the dregs of society.

Soon Anthony chose to make some healthy changes in his life. A year later, he told Mom the night of incarceration was the best thing that ever happened to him.

Teens who are consistently rescued truly believe there will be no consequences to their actions. They have learned there is always someone who will cover for them, make it okay.

On the high school campus, rescuing is a full-blown activity. Teachers rescue. Counselors do it. So do parents. Kids often have a free ride!

I rotate working the attendance department windows at my school. The excuses I've seen—my goodness! Unbelievable. Parents outright lie. If their kid slept in late, the parent writes a note. If their kid isn't ready for a test, he or she doesn't have to come to school. Cutting class is overlooked. The list continues.

On occasion a parent says, "Hey, I'm not excusing my child. He will just have to pay the price for what he has done." I applaud the parent!

My advice is to let your adolescent take his or her lumps. Teenagers must learn responsibility for their actions, and this cannot happen unless they are allowed to experience the adverse ramifications of their behavior.

Around graduation time, I've nicknamed my office "The Wailing Wall." It's the place where the jig is up—the point of no return. Tears flow and promises are made. Too late.

Report cards are mailed home six times a year; parents are written numerous letters; telephone calls are made; students are personally told what they need to graduate—for four years. They are handed referral cards (over and over) to take needed make-up courses in adult school.

About six weeks before graduation, panic sets in. The annual has been ordered and is paid for, so are the announcements. Cap and gown pictures have been taken, expensive new clothes bought, even Grandma's plane ticket purchased.

One piece is missing. The student has multiple courses to complete in adult school as well as passing all the current classes. Time has run out. No way can he or she complete the requirements in time to march across the stage.

It always amazes me how surprised everyone seems to be. There's a magical hope that everything will somehow turn out alright. But it doesn't.

My heart goes out to the student and family in their pain and disappointment. It's difficult to watch the tears cascade down the bronzed cheeks of a 190-pound football player.

These young men and women truly believe someone will give them one more chance. And they're desperately hoping it will be me. Unfortunately for them, it is an impossibility. It's over.

Parents who have rescued their child for years are now faced with the enormous pain it incurred. The end result is not a pretty picture.

In case you're thinking, "Boy, does she ever have a heart of stone," I'll let you in on one of my secrets. Even though these young men and women truly deserve what happened to them, I empathize with their pain and handwrite each of them a letter of encouragement. It's important to me to reassure them as a person and help motivate them to finish their course work in the summer.

Most of my students do just that, and in August I am privileged to give their diploma to them, usually accompanied by a hug. My hope is that they have learned a very difficult lesson through their procrastination.

Rescuing and *support* are two different entities. *Rescuing* is not allowing the teenager to suffer the deserved consequences of his or her actions. *Support* is being there for your teen as an encourager, even though his or her choices were wrong—supporting the person, not the deed.

Chores—the Sure Conflict

"Life's been so tough for me," declared a woman in my therapy office. "My dad and mom just did everything for us. I had no chores or responsibilities to speak of. I never washed, cooked, or cleaned. Nothing. It's been awful trying to catch up and learn skills I should have known."

Not only is it unhealthy for the child, but it is illogical that a parent carry the full workload.

In junior high, one of my daughter's chores was to fold laundry for her dad, herself, and me. She hated it. I was tired of hearing the complaints. *There's got to be a change around here*, I thought.

"Kathi, I've got good news. You won't have to fold the family laundry any longer," I announced. After the jumping up and down and whooping stopped, I added, "You're in junior high now and becoming a young lady; therefore, you will be totally responsible for all your own laundry—wash, dry, fold, hang, and iron."

She wasn't all that thrilled, but she felt it was a lot better than folding laundry for the entire family.

There were a couple of times when I heard, "Mom, where's my new—(blouse, jeans, dress, T-shirt)?" Digging through the hamper, she found it on the bottom. "Hey, how come this wasn't washed? That's what I wanted to wear today."

Or, "I don't have any clean underwear. What am I supposed to wear?"

Empathizing with her, I'd say, "Oh, dear! How awful your clothes are still in the hamper."

Or, "Guess you'll need to dig your underwear out of the hamper and wash them by hand."

Soon Kathi realized I would not rescue her. She either had her clothes laundered and ready, or she had to figure out something else.

She's now a mother with two small children, and their clothes are spotless!

In our society, we no longer wash in the river or use a scrub-board or a wringer washer. Most of us do not even use a clothesline to dry laundry. Doing the wash is a lot easier nowadays.

Teens have the physical and mental ability to put a load in the washer, add soap, and push a button. Drying is even less complicated. Even though it's much easier and cheaper to do all the family wash yourself, it is a disservice for a teen to graduate from high school without being responsible for the care of his or her clothing.

I encourage you to get a new laundry service—your teen.

So once you've decided chores are important for your teen, how do you get him or her to buy into the idea? One way is to allow your teenager to *choose* his or her chores from a list.

"Come on," you're probably saying. "There's no way my kid will do a lick of work, let alone choose something."

It's important to help your adolescent understand that *everyone* will be responsible for certain jobs in the home. After the teen reluctantly chooses several chores, build in the consequences—what will occur if he or she does not do his or her part. Try to make the consequences logical (i.e., no laundry done—no clean clothes to wear). Also, the consequences need to be distasteful, so the teen will not want to continue the behavior.

For instance:

"If the lawns are not mowed by 6:00 P.M. on Saturdays, you will not be allowed to go out with your friends that evening."

"If the bathrooms are not cleaned on Thursday by 6:00 P.M., there will be no T.V. that night."

"If dinner dishes are not cleaned up by 7:00 P.M., Monday through Thursday, you cannot make or receive any phone calls that evening."

Kids soon learn they are unwilling to pay the consequences. They realize it's not worth it.

Another excellent idea was presented by Kathy Mills on a local radio program. At this point, her system has not been published, so I will give a short summary based on recollection. She calls the system "Cleaning for Dollars."

1. Each job has a dollar value.
2. At each job site, there is a card that tells *exactly* what needs to be done, how to do it, and what tools and cleaners to use.

   For example:

   Bathroom

   a. Put (brand name) toilet cleaner in toilet. Use the brush to scrub around the edges and entire bowl.
   b. Put disinfectant on a sponge and go over the outside of the toilet, including the seat and the tank.
   c. Flush the toilet.
   d. Put (brand) cleanser on sponge and clean the basin and bathtub. Rinse with water (using the sponge) until the grit is gone. Squeeze the sponge dry. Wipe dry with sponge. (Extra instructions for the shower.)
   e. Wipe the countertop with (brand) nonscratch cleaner. Rinse sponge in water. Squeeze dry. Wipe counter again with dry sponge. Buff with dry cloth.
   f. Use (brand) glass cleaner to spray the mirror. Wipe dry. Buff with clean, dry cloth.
   g. Vacuum, using power nozzle. Check/clean cobwebs.
   h. Put dirty towels in hamper. Replace with clean towels.

3. Every job has a time limit. Set the timer.

4. When the timer goes off, if the job is complete according to the instructions, the wages are paid.

This plan is unique and valuable in several ways:

- It pays money dividends.
- Each child learns the proper way to clean.
- Dawdling is eliminated by using the timer.

Kathy Mills does not do the cleaning. She sets the timer, supervises, and pays for the services. She stated it costs less than paying a weekly housekeeper, is done the way she expects, and teaches her children the value of the work ethic.

Designer Clothes

Many kids (and adults) have a strong need, based on peer pressure, to wear popular designer labels. Maybe you have noticed—they're expensive.

Barbie looked the part. She was constantly sporting new outfits. Each event called for something special.

"How do you get all these clothes?" I decided to ask.

A giggle escaped her pretty lips. "Well, I just ask Mom," she responded. "Whatever I want, it's okay with her. She gives me the credit card, and I go to the mall." Barbie often charges hundreds of dollars at a whack.

Barbie's mother enjoys pleasing her and having her look pretty. Love is her motive. What she apparently doesn't know is that she is setting her daughter up for some hard times ahead. Barbie has not learned we cannot have everything our hearts desire. She has been taught that instant gratification is the way to go, even if it means charging to the hilt.

None of us, however, want to look weird or out-of-step. Teens, in particular, need to feel they look good.

Here are some ideas for keeping a balance:

Give a clothes allowance. It's best done on a monthly basis. Decide on the amount you feel is equitable. Go shopping a time or two in order to help your (preferably junior high) adolescent make wise choices.

Certain items (winter coat/jacket, boots, school shoes, underwear) are purchased outside the allowance by the parent. Decide on which necessities will be additional.

The teenager will learn how to look for sales, shop at discount stores, and use his or her money wisely.

Occasionally, there may be an item of clothing that will take two months' allowance. Consider giving an advance. When your teen must wait another month for more money, he or she may see that the purchase was not worth it. It will help the teenager to be more discriminating in the future, when he or she feels the sting of the natural consequences.

Teenager pays a fair share. If you have contracted to purchase two pairs of school shoes yearly and your adolescent wants a very expensive pair, you can negotiate.

Teen:	"Dad, I want these (brand) shoes, but they cost $———."
Dad:	"Well, son, I'd like you to have them too. Tell you what I'm willing to do. My budget for shoes is $———. When you have the remainder of the money, I'll be glad to put in my part, and we'll get them."

Adolescent works for additional money. If your child wants more expensive clothes than the budget allows, give opportunity to work for the amount. Consider "Cleaning for Dollars."

The teen can wash windows, clean the garage, wax the car, clean various rooms, reorganize closets, bake, update photo albums, trim bushes and trees, plant flowers, wax floors, cook dinner, polish silverware, bathe the dog, or pull weeds. Use your imagination. Pay only when the job is completed. Or your teen may get a similar job in the neighborhood.

Rescuing your child by allowing an almost unlimited clothes budget is an injustice.

Wheels

Many of the students at my high school lay rubber and scream all over the parking lot with their expensive cars. (It's easy to tell the teachers' parking facilities—the cars are old.) Not only do the kids drive new cars, but generally they are not accountable for gas, upkeep, or insurance. Most of them tell me their parents prefer them not to work.

Unreal!

I would suggest you set aside a designated amount for a car and ask your teen to match it by working. When it has been matched, both of you go car shopping. Also, your teen needs to have a job in order to pay at least half the expenses of insurance, lube and oil jobs, and general upkeep.

Studies show that when a student is given a car, his or her grades plummet. Teenagers, however, who have worked for their car and its maintenance tend to do better in school. They have learned to budget their time and money and are more appreciative.

"Anne's grades are almost all F's since she got her new car on her sixteenth birthday," one mother revealed. "I've talked to her over and over. So have her teachers. I'm at my wits' end. What should I do?"

"Take the car keys," was my suggestion.

"Oh, I couldn't do that," she feebly replied. "Besides, what if she has another set made?"

"Sell the car," I answered.

Mother's mouth flew open, her eyebrows ascended, and she looked as though I had asked her to shoot her offspring.

Getting a better grip on herself, she whispered, "I just can't. There's got to be another way."

There wasn't. Anne did not graduate.

Mom was unwilling to set firm rules for the privilege of car ownership and build in logical consequences when they were ignored. The kid had the auto carte blanche, while Mom wrung her hands.

It is important that the parents—not their irresponsible kid—be in control of the vehicle.

Along with driving cars come traffic tickets and fender benders. Cautious and dependable but inexperienced teens quite often mangle a fender or two. Jay Kesler, in his book *Too Big to Spank*, suggests the parent pay the *first* fender bender, as well as the *first* ticket. This act of kindness will show our adolescents that we understand their inexperience, are willing to back them up, and cut them a little slack. Most teenagers will respond by becoming reliable drivers.

The Big *T*

Telephones.

Kids have been almost hermetically attached to telephones since the days they jiggled the receiver up and down for the operator. Nowadays, I've observed several students (and parents) talking on a cellular phone while waiting to see their high school counselor—me.

Today teenagers and telephones are almost synonymous. Not only do they see most of their friends all day at school, they have a great need to be on the phone half the night discussing the same stuff they talked about during the day.

Seventh grade flashes back into my memory. It was *vital* I call my friend as soon as I got in the house. (We had just walked home together.) It was important to talk over what we were going to wear the next day (sweater and skirt—same thing we wore every day). Incidentally, it was nearly one hundred degrees, but we insisted on wearing our new winter school clothes, even though the California winter was two months away. Then we blabbed on and on about momentous topics—cute boys.

Phone conversations are important to kids, especially girls, and can be a healthy outlet when it is not out of control. Since teenagers aren't terrific with self-restriction, parents need to set the limits. Here are some ideas:

1. Decide on the number of phone calls each day.
2. Set a time limit (either per phone call or total time of all calls).
3. Telephone usage is a privilege. Choose when it may be utilized (for instance, after dinner, following completion of homework, when chores are done).
4. Decide who answers incoming calls.
5. The teen pays for any long-distance calls he or she makes.

When (not if) the adolescent chooses to ignore the telephone limits, logical consequences will occur (i.e., no outgoing or incoming calls for two days).

It's easier for everyone concerned to install a phone in the adolescent's bedroom. However, *I'm totally against the idea.* Monitoring becomes nearly impossible. The teen is also more apt to feel violated when the parent wishes to set limits. A power struggle can ensue. Save yourself the hassle. Nix the bedroom phone.

Godly Fathers—Rescued Sons

The Bible describes several parents who rescued their children to death. Eli was a respected priest in Israel. He raised his charge, little Samuel, in the actual house of God. Righteously. But his own sons (Hophni and Phinehas) committed horrendous deeds—right there in the temple (1 Sam. 2:22–25).

Now you would think since Samuel observed all this while growing up, he would have been quite different with his own offspring. But his sons, Joel and Abijah, took bribes and perverted justice. A group of elders even talked to Samuel about them (1 Sam. 8:1–5). It was too late. Samuel's rescuing produced corrupt sons.

Then there was King David, a man after God's own heart. His son Amnon raped Tamar, his half-sister. Even though David was very angry, he refused to confront his son. Later Amnon was killed on his brother Absalom's order (2 Sam. 13:1–29). Then, spoiled Absalom also went on to disgrace his father and died an early death.

Godly men who were brokenhearted over their children's debauchery. Irresponsible, ungodly sons whom the fathers had rescued.

In Conclusion

Rescuing is the easy road. Accountability is not. It takes guts, stamina, and consistency. Whether it's limiting phone calls, refusing to write notes to the school to get your child off the hook, insisting on chores, or leaving him or her in jail overnight, it's important to not give our kids free rein but to allow them to suffer the consequences of their actions.

Proverbs 19:19 suggests an angry person must be responsible for the consequences, and that "if you rescue him, you will only have to do it again." The admonition of allowing logical consequences and refusing to rescue could certainly be applied to teenagers.

It is unlikely that there is a parent alive who does not want to be appreciated by his or her children—eventually. Even though it's on hold for a few years, parents want to believe it will inevitably occur.

If you want your kids to forget you when they are adults, give them their hearts' desires during the growing-up years.

Rescue them, require no accountability, and take away the repercussions for their deeds. Children who are given too much learn to be stingy and unappreciative and think the world owes them their ultimate yearnings. They believe society should revolve around their needs and wishes. How unrealistic.

God has put us in the position of guiding our children, and they deserve a parent who loves them enough to get out of the rescuing game.

Coming to Grips

1. In what ways do you rescue your child? List them.
   ____
   ____
   ____
   ____

2. Now rank them in the order of importance.
   a. ____________________________________
   b. ____________________________________
   c. ____________________________________
   d. ____________________________________

3. If you are married, share your list with your spouse. Ask for input.

4. Choose one area (probably the first one on the list) on which you will concentrate.

5. Decide to work on the entire list—one by one.

5

Exploring Your Parenting Style

"Okay, kid," we bellow, "I've had it with you. Go to your room—until you're eighteen. We'll slide the food under the door."

Or,

"Well, I'm not so sure about your going to the heavy metal concert. I mean you're only fourteen, and the driver just got his license last week. I know all your friends are going. Well, I guess it would be all right. Just this once."

We can come off sounding like a drill sergeant or a wimp. Sometimes both. Let's take a closer look at parenting styles: *controlling*, *permissive*, *neglectful*, and *assertive*.

Controlling

The controlling parenting style is *strong on control* and *weak on support*. It's the "shape up or ship out" method. The drill sergeant.

It seemed like I counseled the Tanner family for ten years. There were five children, and every year or so there was a new one entering high school.

Mrs. Tanner hit the office like a whirlwind when her firstborn came to high school. Demand, demand, demand. There was always something wrong. She didn't like the school, the teachers, the students, or me. We were all imperfect.

My first glimpse of Bob was that of an insecure, scared boy. He couldn't look me in the eye and sat curled in a fetal position as Mom raged about what had happened Bob's first day in high school.

At first most freshmen are frightened, overwhelmed, uncomfortable, and they wish they could go back to junior high. They don't know where the classes are, and they are scared to death to ask anyone—especially an awesome senior.

Bob got in line to purchase his student body card. As he nervously shifted from one foot to the other, his book bag slipped off one shoulder and was instantly grabbed by an upperclassman. Gleefully, and at the expense of Bob, it was thrown back and forth, the contents flying everywhere. Bob tried desperately to get it by flailing his arms awkwardly, but with no success. Soon the game stopped and Bob carefully put his belongings back into the bag.

Mom was furious. She basically wanted the culprits strung up and hung from the flagpole. Now!

"You should have stood up for yourself," she bellowed at meek Bob. "You know that bag cost a bundle, and you let those boys practically ruin it. Wait until you ever get another one. No, sir, I'm not putting out money for you anymore. You're weak and disgusting."

Through successive children, Mom continued to blow off steam at the school as well as wallop her kids. Their self-esteem was beaten down. Destroyed.

The Tanner children were some of the nicest students, yet they were incapable of doing much for themselves. They had been crippled by a controlling parent.

Parents who excessively control often make wimps out of their kids. These adolescents do not learn how to approach a teacher for extra help, ask questions, challenge a grade, solicit guidance from their counselor, or stand up for themselves with their peers. They remind me of lost children.

The controlling parenting style strips children of individuality. Their self-esteem is low, and they often become people pleasers. They do not want to be like their parent, so they give up their life to the control of others. Anyone.

Often they do not feel eligible for the good things in life. These controlled teenagers are submissive but do not feel loved.

Some teenagers react to a controlling parent very differently. They rebel. I've witnessed scores of these adolescents thumb their noses at their parents and take off. Some run away to drugs, alcohol, unlawful acts, sleazy friends, and promiscuity. It appears they want to show their parents they will live as they wish. Usually, it's a very damaging lifestyle.

Some who appear to be the dregs of society are tender children inside. I've touched their hearts and seen their pain when I've allowed them to talk, cry, and scream. I sense the damage is very deep. They have a great need for their parent—an urgent desire to be loved.

Emmy was from a fine home from all the outward appearances. Through the first two years of high school she did well, was obedient, and seemed rather shy.

Dad was an overly controlling parent. He called the shots. Emmy's desires were not considered, because he knew what was best for his child. Often he was either in my office or on the telephone demanding just about everything. He bulldozed his way to the top. No one was going to stop him from getting what he wanted. This man could strike fear in most people. His wife and children submitted—in terror.

I could hardly believe my eyes when I saw Emmy at the beginning of eleventh grade. Total turnaround. Her makeup and dress depicted the style of the extremely rebellious student population. She was dating a boy whom her parents hated. She managed to fail nearly every course. I suspected she was on drugs. Near the end of the school year, she was reported as a runaway.

Her father came into my office to report the sad news. Tears slipped over his cheeks as he related the story. He was the picture of a broken, beaten man.

"Mrs. Gordon, I wanted to tell you where I am," Emmy's voice whispered over the telephone. "I'm in Los Angeles."

"Emmy, are you living on the streets?" I questioned.

"Uh-huh," was her reply.

"How are you getting money for food?" I continued.

No response.

"Emmy, I have a feeling you're prostituting. Is that right?" I ventured.

"Yes," she softly answered. "I know it's terrible, but I can't stand my parents any longer. My dad would never allow me to be a person. I had to get away from his control."

Emmy's parents loved her deeply, and their heartbreak was gut-wrenching. Her father believed he was doing what was best for his daughter by strict, rigid control. Even though he would literally die for her, he seemed incapable of expressing his love in ways other than domination.

Fortunately, not all children of controlling parents are to the extremes of Bob and Emmy. Nonetheless, overpowering is detrimental to the adolescent and stunts normal growth toward adulthood.

Parents have told me, "When my children graduate from high school, then I'll let them make their own choices." But I have observed parents of mature, adult children (now in their thirties and forties) continuing in a ruling posture. A sheepskin doesn't do it.

Permissive

These parents are *strong on support* but *weak on control*. Rescuing is the normal forte—always letting the kid off the hook, making sure everything turns out okay, fixing and fixing again. Interesting how protecting parents feel so noble.

Overly supportive parents may feel guilty if they, or someone else, mete out discipline. They have a difficult time standing back and allowing their teenagers to suffer the consequences of their choices. Therefore, they rescue.

Sometimes parents give in because the adolescent is so out-of-control, life becomes nearly unbearable. The kid is bent on having his or her own way—regardless. This kind of teen can make it tough on a parent by haranguing and continual, blatant disobedience. So "peace at any price" may become the parent's motto.

Not only may the child of a permissive home environment have low self-esteem and feel emotionally unsupported, but he or she often thinks society will turn his or her poor decisions into wonderful consequences. This teen believes the world owes it to him or her.

Most incoming ninth graders are polite and scared. Whatever I (or any adult) say usually goes. They don't do a lot of questioning. However, there are plenty of exceptions. I can't count the times I've heard a teenager say, "I have my rights!" *Your rights?* I think. *Hey, you're only fourteen. Get real.*

With humor I recall a little ninth grade teenybopper. Her hair was cut in a childlike style, which made her look even younger. Stretching her body toward the ceiling, she placed her hands on her hips and loudly announced, "I have my rights, and I demand some changes around this school." It was hard not to laugh.

What was humorous about her as a young freshman gradually became more irritating as she neared graduation. Nothing was ever right, and she took every opportunity to point out the problems. Unfortunately, she overlooked the biggest aggravation—herself.

Throughout the years, it was easier for the parents to yield to the wishes of their daughter, but their permissiveness became detrimental to her in the long run.

Teenagers need direction and discipline in order to feel good about themselves, set goals, and persevere.

Neglectful

Low support is coupled with *low control* in this parenting style. It appears to be the most common style in our affluent society.

Children of a neglectful home are apt to have the lowest self-image of the group. There is a feeling of, "What's the use; no one cares, so I'll ——— (get drunk, take drugs, be promiscuous, run away)."

Ricky came to my school in the middle of his sophomore year. I could hardly believe my eyes when I looked at his records. Since beginning high school in ninth grade, he had entered and left eight schools. He lived with Mom, who moved often, then was sent to Dad, and ended up living with an uncle.

He was a kid who had little parental control or concern. It was as though he were a nonentity—most domestic animals have better care. The family, including the uncle, paid little attention to him. He was left to fend for himself, which he was doing. Badly.

Ricky came often to my office for support, encouragement, and therapy. Even though we had an excellent bond, sometimes I felt I would never get through to him. Yet he began to improve, and he ended the year with decent grades.

Two more times Ricky was forced to move to another school. Each time he lost credits for graduation and seemed to give up.

Finally, Ricky was allowed to stay put in my school during his senior year. He was far behind, beaten down, with little drive or self-respect, but we worked out a rigorous schedule for graduation. It was almost second semester before he began to implement the plan. Unfortunately, graduation did not occur.

The June sun was deep into the western horizon following graduation. I felt a strong arm gently pull me into a half-hug. Ricky's sad and tear-stained face told the story. "I never thought it would hurt so much not to graduate," he whispered.

"Mrs. Gordon, remember me?" Ricky almost shouted as he burst into my office.

"Oh, my!" I returned. "How long has it been? Tell me what you're doing now."

"Three years since I've seen you," Ricky responded. "You won't believe what I have to tell you. Your words finally got through to me, and I completed my classes and graduated from adult school. I'm finishing my second year in a

Christian college and am an assistant to a youth pastor. That's what I want to do when I graduate. I'm also thinking of seminary."

My heart was deeply touched, and my broad smile gave way to glistening tears.

"I became a Christian because of you," he continued. "You were the one person who believed in me and cared what happened."

These teenage success stories are abundant. They are the ones who make my job rewarding and encourage me to continue a hard task. I could fill chapters with their stories. Tears well up as I remember these precious teens. It seems God brings them across my path to be loved and guided. I am truly grateful and feel it is a divine privilege to work with these unloved, neglected adolescents.

On the brighter side, most parents are not *deliberately* neglectful. In our whirlwind society/lifestyle, it is easy to succumb to the urgent and neglect the important—our kids. Sometimes parents neglect their offspring because they have little strength to do anything different.

Parents come home from work dead tired. A little peace and quiet is all they ask. They just can't stand another problem or another request. So they hide—behind a newspaper, in front of a television, in a book, in a phone conversation, even in the bathroom—whatever it takes to get away. It becomes a habit. Eventually the teen no longer asks or expects anything. He or she becomes a lost child.

Another way a parent neglects is by giving in to the wishes of the adolescent. Children of all ages are generally selfish individuals. They have nothing better to do than think of ways to either overpower or break down their parent in order to get what they want.

Probably every parent in America at one time or another has given in. We can't stand the harassment. It's easier to allow the teen to do what he or she wishes.

Isn't it interesting how soon teenagers catch on. Before long they make a big deal out of everything. They know if they keep it up long enough, their parents will fold, and they will have their self-centered heart's desire. A pattern has reared its ugly head—giving the adolescents what they want. The teenagers like it, at first. Eventually, though, they feel neglected and unloved because parental boundaries have been removed.

As people who are trying to be excellent, we slip into unhealthy parenting styles. Sometimes we are controlling, then the pendulum swings to permissive, or we are neglectful. It would be wonderful if we were consistently using good parenting techniques, but we habitually slide.

In talking with scores of parents, men tend to be more controlling, whereas women tend toward permissiveness. Yet I've seen my share of wimpy men and witchy women, so there are exceptions.

Assertive

In working with thousands of adolescents and their parents, I have found that the vast majority of parents want to consistently deal with their children in a productive, kind manner. The assertive style is one in which the child *feels loved yet controlled*. Of all the styles, this one produces more high self-esteem and self-worth in the offspring. It's the one for which we aim.

Karen and her brother, Joel, were known among the high school faculty as "those Beatty kids." This was not meant to be a compliment. They were two years apart in age and grade, and they came from a divorced home. They cut classes regularly, showed up late, were discipline problems, received lots of detention and Saturday school, and failed most courses.

With my encouragement and an administrator's threat of sending him to continuation high school (an alternative half-day program at another site), Joel buckled down the last semester and *almost* graduated.

Recently I received a call from him. "Hey, Mrs. Gordon, I finished the four classes I needed this summer, and I'm coming down for my diploma."

Karen began a turnaround as well. In a summer conference with her and her father (both Joel and Karen live with a neglectful mother), we went over the June report card. Previously Karen failed most classes, but this time she had one C—the rest were D's.

I was expecting Dad to be all over her.

Instead, he put his arm around her and gave a squeeze. Looking directly into her eyes, he said, "Honey, I'm so proud of you. Look at those grades. This is the best report card you have ever had." Karen's embarrassed response was a giggle. She beamed.

Rarely, if ever, have I heard a parent congratulating a child on D grades. Yet, this father acknowledged improvement and was truly excited about it. I resisted the urge to hug him!

I'm willing to bet this year Karen will do better than ever. She has a dad who is concerned about her self-esteem and wants her to feel loved. She does.

It takes a lot of self-control, guts, and perseverance to be an assertive parent. It's essential to

listen to our kids (chapter 1)
look realistically at the issues
set limits and stick to them (chapter 2)

respect our children's personhood
discipline appropriately—not punish (chapter 3)
stop the rescuing game (chapter 4)
prepare our children for adulthood (chapter 12)
be a godly example (chapter 13)

Just in case you've adopted an exaggerated view of my ability to handle kids, here's some honesty that will quickly dispel the myth.

The start of school is lovingly called "Hell Week." With over six hundred counselees, some of the days I've seen a teenager every three to five minutes. That's stress.

Each kid has something wrong with his or her schedule. Most of the time it's legitimate. Other times it's:

"I don't want P.E. in the morning; it's cold."
"My lunch is too late."
"The teacher wants me to work in this class."
"My friend and I want a different class."
"When I swim in P.E., my hair falls out."

I've heard the unbelievable. Then there's the teen who has had one or two program changes already and comes back whining for another one. It gets to me.

Lynn was a little ninth grader who already had two program changes and came with a note from a teacher for *another* change. (Many students moan and cry to a teacher to be in or out of a class, and the kind teacher complies with a note to me.) This time, it slung me into orbit.

"You've had two program changes, Lynn. No more," I crankily spit out. I didn't even read the teacher's note.

"When can I come back?" she shyly asked.

"When you're in tenth grade," I stormed.

After she headed out the door, I read the note. She was in a class reserved for sophomores—misplaced. Computer error. I ran after her.

"Lynn, this is my fault, and I'm truly sorry. I had no right to not read the note or to treat you unkindly. This is not your problem. It's our blunder." I gave her a hug.

Here sat this frightened little girl, unsure of high school, thrown out of a class by a teacher, and handled disrespectfully by her counselor. I felt awful.

How important it is to nurture, love, and train our children. We all want what is best for our kids, and we desperately desire to be superior parents. Because of this, we have a great responsibility to continue to grow in our parenting skills.

There will be days when we blow it. At those times, it's critical to approach our offended child in honesty. Take the blame. No excuses. Call it what it is—wrong. Ask for forgiveness.

Then go on being the best parent we can.

Coming to Grips

For insight on your parenting style, take the following test. Think through each sentence to determine whether it's similar to the way you tend to respond to your teenager. Write down whether you have this attitude:

O—Often
S—Sometimes
N—Almost Never

____ 1. "Don't bother me now. You'll do okay."
____ 2. "Hey, kid, shape up or ship out."

____ 3. "You look upset. Tell me what's wrong."

____ 4. "Let me be clear about the rules. It's my way or the highway."

____ 5. "I'd like to support you in buying your first car. Whatever you earn in the next year, I will put in an equal amount."

____ 6. "I've told you over and over, this is the last time I'm spending this much money on designer clothes."

____ 7. "Quit your bellyaching. Act like a man."

____ 8. "Stop your moping around. It's just puppy love."

____ 9. "Well, just this once. But don't ask to go to another heavy metal concert."

____ 10. "If it weren't for you kids, I'd be a success. I'm stuck with a ghastly life."

____ 11. "I can understand you forgot to call, but two hours past curfew is just too late. Try to do better."

____ 12. "Because I said so, that's why."

____ 13. "Curfew was up an hour ago. I understand you forgot to call; therefore, you have earned the consequences of staying home next Saturday night."

____ 14. "When I want your input, I'll ask. Get it?"

____ 15. "I guess it won't hurt if you drive around the block; after all, you'll be getting your permit soon."

____ 16. "Whatever."

____ 17. "I hate to say 'no' when all your friends have one."

____ 18. "I'm busy."

____ 19. "We had a deal that the car would be washed by 5:00 tonight. Since you have chosen not to abide by our contract, you cannot use the car this evening."

____ 20. "I've always admired your intelligence. These grades are not even average and are unacceptable. Let's brainstorm a plan for improvement, then you will be accountable to me to work the plan."

Scoring Parenting Styles

Under each section, write the number of O's, S's, and N's:

NEGLECTFUL
Sentences 1, 8, 10, 16, 18
______O ______S ______N

PERMISSIVE
Sentences 6, 9, 11, 15, 17
______O ______S ______N

CONTROLLING
Sentences 2, 4, 7, 12, 14
______O ______S ______N

ASSERTIVE
Sentences 3, 5, 13, 19, 20
______O ______S ______N

Usually a pattern will emerge. The more responses you have in a particular area, the more you tend to use that style of parenting. Also, a mix of two distinct styles could materialize.

Concentrate on your areas of strength as an assertive parent (listen, be realistic, set limits that stick, respect your child, discipline appropriately, stop rescuing, be a godly example).

Conversely, work on weaker traits from the other styles (neglectful, permissive, and controlling).

Parenting—Then 'n' Now

1. What did you need from your parent that you did *not* get?
   Mom ____________________
   Dad ____________________

2. What method could your parents have used to more effectively discipline you?
   Mom ____________________
   Dad ____________________

3. What discipline/punishment did *not* work? ________
   ____
   ____

4. How did they handle your anger (and other emotions)?
   Mom ____________________
   Dad ____________________

5. Name a discipline method you hated as a child. ______
   ____

   Do you hear yourself saying/doing the same things your parents said/did? ____________________
   ____

6. Which of your children is most like you in temperament? (Ask your spouse, relative, or close friend.)
   ____

   What is the most effective way to work with this child? ____________________
   ____
   ____

6

The Little Red Schoolhouse

Picture the one-room schoolhouse of yesteryear. The wooden bucket standing stately in the corner with the dipper ready for young lips to taste spring water. A switch, too, awaiting a naughty child's bottom. Girls in pigtails—boys with frogs in their pockets. A wood-burning stove with the big black pipe extending through the ceiling. Inkwells.

This portrait conjures up nostalgic scenes of what schools and children were like in a simpler, less complex era. But no more. Most high schools are no longer uncomplicated, and the rules are constantly changing.

But there's hope!

Parental Encouragement

Gino is one of the kids I consider "lost." My heart goes out to these teens, and I desperately try to motivate them and let them know I believe in them.

"Hey, Gino," I urged him in his junior year. "The football coach said he really wants you to play football next year. You will need to pass all your classes and make up English and World History this summer to be eligible."

"Yeah, well, I don't know," Gino responded.

"You don't want to play football?" I questioned.

"Sorta," he returned.

"What does that mean, Gino?" I continued.

"My parents have never seen me play." He averted his eyes, slumped lower in the chair, nervously cleared his throat, then mumbled, "They haven't been to even one game in three years. If they don't care, why should I?"

In Gino I sensed a discouraged, damaged teen with a what's-the-use attitude. He did not pass all his courses nor did he take classes in the summer. I saw his mother for the first time when she came to check him out midway through his senior year.

I acknowledge that adolescents have a weird way of showing their parents they want them to attend their events (sports, band, drama, academic achievements, open house). Most of the time, they act as though they could not care less or even tell their parents to stay home.

Just the opposite is true. No matter how your teen acts—be there! Underneath, it means a great deal to your child.

If you are able to be involved with the school in a helpful way, I encourage you to do so. Join booster clubs for the various sports events, band, drama. Drive kids to club outings, bake cookies, sell stuff.

Kids like their parents to be involved and interested in their pursuits. It spells *love*.

The Big G—Grades

A friend and I chose to take a conversational Spanish class several years ago for no grade/no credit. Because I didn't have to push for a grade, I did little studying or memorizing. On the way to class, I'd steer my car with one hand, conjugate verbs, and try to keep from hitting another motorist. The next semester, I took the class for a grade and credit. I learned a lot.

Whether it's good or bad, our society gives grades as rewards. Quite honestly, grades make or break a high schooler's chances of entering the college of his or her choice.

I received an unusual telephone call. "Mrs. Gordon, I have a very serious matter to discuss with you," stated the caller. "I am one who reviews prospective students for U.S.C., and I'm very disturbed about a letter enclosed with the application of one of your students."

She read aloud a letter that ended, "Unless I am admitted to U.S.C., I will commit suicide."

The letter was from Bill, an intense, quiet, and desperate student.

When I called him in, he volunteered, "My parents want nothing less than straight A's and admission to U.S.C. I'm so scared I won't be able to live up to their expectations."

Fortunately, Bill was able to talk through his feelings and view life with a healthier perspective.

Thankfully, this was an isolated incident. However, some parents tend to put great stock into the grades their children earn.

Here are some tips on grades: Most schools give grades every six to nine weeks. Call the school to find out the schedule. Then mark your calendar accordingly. Usually it takes one week to ten days for the grades to be in your mailbox.

If the grades are not there:

1. Call the school to see if your child has an unpaid bill.
2. Confront your teen about either not bringing them home or taking them from the mailbox.
3. Check the grades carefully; some kids change them.

Often, in the remarks section, a teacher will make a comment. If the teacher asks you to call him or her, oblige.

Some parents want the teachers to continually call for low grades, no homework, cutting classes, and so forth. They are parents who are genuinely interested in their child's progress and want to know what's going on. However, high school teachers have nearly two hundred students per day. It becomes an overwhelming task to keep in touch with all the parents. Because of the large size of high school classes, students are expected to take more responsibility. Teachers, however, are usually more than willing to return a parent's telephone call.

One way of keeping on top of grades is to have your student take a progress sheet to each teacher on Friday. The teacher can quickly check off the student's progress (approximate grade, attendance, homework completion, and student attitude). Most schools supply the form for the asking; if not, make your own.

Encourage your child. If his or her grade increases from an F to a D—be excited. Praise him or her. Parental admiration will encourage your teen to try even harder.

It was one of those conferences! The parent was coming in to talk about her daughter's grades—all F's. I dreaded it. However, when we looked at the new progress report card, Cindy's mom hugged her and said, "Look honey, you only have one F. I'm really proud of you." Cindy giggled with delight as she looked into the face of her proud mother.

One last thing on grades. It goes against my professional judgment for a parent to pay for good grades. So many bucks per A is ridiculous. Of course there are always exceptions. If your child has consistently earned D's and F's, offer him or her a total sum of money or a special outing for a specific improvement (e.g., "If you have no F's on your next report card.")

AWOL

As the brilliant sun sparkled in the September morn, a tiny five-year-old ran out the front door with his brand-new lunch pail, ready to greet the academic world. Mom had carefully chosen the outfit, brushed his hair until it gleamed, and scrubbed his teeth to a pearl finish. His dancing eyes matched the excitement of his feet. He had waited five long years for this day.

For a lot of children, however, school begins to lose its luster as the years continue. *Playing hooky* was a pastime for youngsters in the 1800s. Kids met at the ol' fishin' hole. Later, it was called *skipping school;* now it's just plain *cutting*.

Consistent nonattendance is serious, and parents and schools should be greatly concerned. In my thinking, it's vital that parents keep on top of the whereabouts of their children. So here is a surefire way to stop cutting. It takes a lot of parental courage, but it is well worth the effort.

Sit your teenager down for a talk:

Parent:	"You have been cutting classes. This is totally unacceptable behavior."
Teen:	(Thinks, *Big deal!*)
Parent:	"I will call the attendance office every Friday to see if you have missed any school."
Teen:	(Rolls eyes.)

Parent: "If you have cut class, you will be accountable to me as to where you were and what you were doing."

Teen: (Thinks, *Get real!*)

Parent: "The following week I will again call the attendance office on Friday. If you have missed even one class, I will take off work the next Monday and walk you to the door of every class."

Teen: (Thinks, *Sure you will. Uh-huh.*)

Working the plan:

1. Set the scene for your teenager. State *exactly* what you expect. Build in the *consequences* (you will walk him or her to the door of each class).
2. Call the attendance office on Friday (or whatever day you chose).
3. When your adolescent gets home from school, confront him or her about the missed classes.

Parent: "Jim, I called the attendance office today. You missed second and third periods on Tuesday, all day Thursday, and first period today. Where were you?"

Teen: "Hey, Mom, the school's records are wrong. I'm there every single day. Just ask any of my friends. Get off my back!"

Parent: "I will call the attendance office again on Friday, Jim, and if you have missed any more classes, I will walk you to the door of each class on Monday."

Teen: "Whatever!"

4. If your child is still cutting classes the next week, telephone the school and let the counselor know you will

be at school Monday to walk your teen to the door of each class. The counselor will very likely be supportive. If not, do it anyway.

5. Get up early Monday and get ready. Take your truant child to school and walk him or her to the door of the first class. Be at the door when the bell rings to end the period. Walk your teen to the next class, etc.

Fred was a football player, about six-foot-two-inches and close to two hundred pounds. His mom was a foot shorter—and gutsy.

Her son consistently cut classes and was a habitual liar. His stories were some of the most ingenious I've ever heard. Mom and I talked over the plan, and she decided to go for it.

"This will be a long, difficult day for you," I said. "Bring something to do, eat, and drink during class time, and you may stay in our faculty lounge. I'll give you a campus map and time schedule of classes so you will know when to be at the door."

This mom was determined. Looking out my window, I saw her son bolt out the door toward his next class, taking long, fast strides. Mom was jogging to keep up. No way would she let him get away from her.

Later he told his mom, "I've never been so humiliated in my whole life." But Fred chose to end his cutting career—so did his sister!

It's highly unlikely you will need to do it twice.

In a parent conference recently, the parents were wringing their hands over a son who was failing, cutting school, and writing his own excuse notes. I gave my plan to end truancy to the father. He thought it was marvelous.

The next week he called to say, "My son is still cutting."

"Have you implemented the plan I suggested?" I asked.

"Well," he responded, "I thought I would call the assistant principal to see if he had any other ideas."

Within three weeks, his son was sent involuntarily to a continuation high school by the assistant principal.

Most parents are unwilling to use such drastic measures to keep their child in school. I understand it's hard, but for those who have had the intestinal fortitude to go from class to class with their adolescent, they are convinced of its value. So are the kids!

Discipline—Then and Now

Years ago when a kid got a lickin' at school, he got one at home too. Parents backed up the school.

Some parents still do. I've heard a multitude of parents say, "Whatever discipline you want to give, I'm behind you 100 percent." They are willing for their child to take whatever consequences are deserved. Usually they will also say, "Believe me, my teen and I will have some dialogue tonight." Usually a subdued kid comes to school the next day. These parents are not afraid of their children—no matter how big they are. They are willing to be a parent, even when it's difficult.

Other parents protect their kids. They believe the school is totally wrong, so is the teacher, and especially the counselor. "You can bet I'll be taking this to the board of education. I'll have your job!" they threaten.

On a happier note, of the thousands of adolescents and parents I have worked with, the vast majority are respectful, appreciative, and kind.

Adam was a new student to me. He was a tenth grader, and when my counseling load increased, I got him. When I first talked to him, I thought, *What a neat kid.*

Then he came on a discipline referral. The teacher was furious. Adam was flagrantly disruptive and defiant.

"Well, Adam, I need to give you an hour detention," I said.

"Who do you think you are?" he screamed. "I won't do any detention, and if I'm suspended, that's great. I have my rights! You just sit here and collect your check; you make me sick."

"Now it's two hours of detention because of your disrespect," I responded. "Since you do not have a sixth period, if you wish you may sit it out in my office for one hour, then go to the detention room for the other hour. If not, you may do one hour each day."

After he left my office, my secretary said, "His sister is just like him."

The next afternoon, a different Adam quietly came to my door. "I'm here to do the detention," he said. "Also, I apologize for the way I talked to you yesterday. Those things I said were not true; I was just mad."

Frankly, I wasn't expecting the positive response I received from Adam. We were then able to spend time talking about the root of his anger issues.

In justly meting out discipline, my purpose is to bring about attitude change in a kind and fair manner. On the first referral, I choose not to call the parent, because I'm hoping the student and I can work it out. Most of the time we do.

My goal for many years is that each time I must discipline students, they will say, "Thank you" when they leave my office. Rarely does it not happen. I want the students to feel they have been treated impartially and with respect.

There have been a few times I've been unfair with a student. Most often it was because I did not know all the circumstances, and I jumped the gun. When I am wrong, I have no problem reversing whatever disciplinary action I inaccurately gave.

If you believe your child was treated unfairly, go to the school personnel concerned and express your feelings. If it is done in an honest, palatable way, most people will respond positively. Teachers and counselors also greatly appreciate your approaching them first before going over their head. Do not repress something that greatly concerns either you or your child.

Fun Classes

Teenagers need courses that spark their interest. Balance is a vital part of life, making the dull things more bearable.

Some classes that include extracurricular involvement are drama, band, choir, sports, journalism, yearbook. These courses are exciting, keep your teen busy doing worthwhile activities, and are great learning experiences.

Even the nonacademic who dislikes school can find his or her niche. Teenagers will learn to read, do mathematical equations, and write when they are taking a vocational course, because it is incorporated into the process of learning the job skill. The by-product of learning a trade is academic knowledge.

A popular course in my high school is elementary aide. Over fifty students work with teachers and children at the elementary school across the street. They work with students in small groups (reading, math, science), teach students to paste, color, play ball—whatever activities are going on during the day.

Most of the elementary aide students are noncollege oriented. In fact, a number of them are disenchanted with school. Yet I've watched teenagers on the playground with six kids hanging all over them. They are thoroughly enjoying themselves—feeling needed, wanted, and loved.

Many academically disinterested teens have made turnarounds because they have found a purpose.

Alternative Learning Programs

Most school districts offer an array of alternative educational opportunities. Here are a few:

Summer school has been around since kids started flunking classes. Now it's also offered for acceleration or enrichment courses.

Community colleges often have head-start programs for those students working toward the university. Courses are offered evenings and during summers. The student has the choice of using the grade and credit for high school or for college (not both).

Adult schools offer academic make-up courses in the afternoons and evenings, along with a wide range of vocational programs.

Independent study (sometimes called home study) is one where the student meets with a designated teacher for assignments and explanation, then completes twenty hours of work at home. The student must be able to work independently and be self-motivated.

Continuation high school is another alternative. Most students attend four hours daily (morning or afternoon session) earning one credit for each fifteen hours of completed work until they acquire the credits needed.

R.O.P. (Regional Occupational Program) is a California program that offers vocational courses in the community. Students get unpaid, on-the-job training in a wide range of occupations (e.g., bank teller, florist, travel agent, dental assistant, model, vet assistant, nurse's aide, farm hand) and earn high school credits. This is also an excellent way for a student to try out an occupation.

The G.E.D. (General Educational Development) is available nationwide for students who are eighteen years old and wish to leave high school prior to graduation. It is a high school *equivalency*—not a diploma. A G.E.D., however, will meet requirements for community college entrance, military service enlistment, and employment.

Some states have a *proficiency examination* (similar to G.E.D.) for those wishing to leave high school before the legal age requirement.

Contact your local school district for alternative programs offered in your area.

"Senioritis"

As a form of rebellion, a troubled teenager may earn poor grades and become a possible nongrad. So I encourage parents to *remove their reason to rebel.*

Sit your adolescent down in his or her senior year (never earlier) and say, "I want you to graduate. If you do, I'll be in the first row grinning from ear to ear and cheering. If you choose not to graduate, it won't diminish my love for you.

"So, I'm officially off your back. You are no longer accountable to me for what you choose to do in school. You have my permission to fail classes, earn poor grades, or not graduate. It's totally up to you. If you want my encouragement, I'm here for you. However, your graduation is your responsibility."

Scores of times I've encouraged parents to say these words to their teen. These same parents, who have been wringing their hands for several years and promising, "I'll do anything—just tell me what to do," turn pale and nearly pass out when they hear my recommendation.

Almost without exception, the parents who have guts enough to back off from their teenager's graduation (grades, school attendance, etc.) will jubilantly watch their child walk across the stage to receive that coveted diploma.

Recently, there were ten possible nongrad students in my counseling load. Six of the parents gritted their teeth, allowed their adolescents total responsibility over their graduation, and hoped that I was right. Their children graduated.

Four other parents agreed with my philosophy but would not let go. None of their children graduated with their class.

When teens have full accountability for their own graduation, they usually decide it's what they want. Then, they work like crazy and get it done.

Working with Teachers, Counselors, Administrators

A palm plant given by a grateful mother grows in my kitchen window. Occasionally I have received a call or note from a parent expressing appreciation. These are the kindnesses that helped me stick with a tough, often thankless job. When a parent has complimented me, I jokingly suggest they put it in writing—to the principal. I'm serious.

Conversely, counselors are often the brunt of abuse, since they are the first line of defense at the high school level. There are some parents who are rude, scream obscenities, threaten, and are so disrespectful their vile words cannot be put into print. Sometimes it is very discouraging.

Educators are highly skilled professional people. Yet not all are excellent teachers, counselors, or administrators. But in working with hundreds of professionals, I believe *most* of them are dedicated people and want the best for your child.

Most parents will need, at some time, to talk with a faculty member about a grade that appears inaccurate, an incorrect class placement, a teacher-student conflict, or school policy—to name a few. When the school personnel is approached in honesty, gentleness, and a desire to work it out, it is a rare professional who will not listen to the parents and do what he or she can to alleviate the situation. Conversely, demanding, critical parents will be ignored or, at best, given little consideration.

However, when you need to go up the chain of command, most school personnel have no problem. In fact, I have encouraged parents to continue trying when they feel strongly about a situation. I believe in the parents' right to fight for their children. When we work *with* school personnel, we can usually work out the problems.

Little Green Apples

Green apples are my favorite. Biting into an apple, hearing it crackle as my teeth puncture the skin and pull out the meat, and feeling the juice escape from the corners of my mouth is a delightful part of autumn.

When I was four years old, we had an apple tree in the backyard. Summer was warm, the trees were in full bloom, yet the apples were small and green. My mom explained that I had to wait until they were red. I'd waited for days. No change. I became impatient.

Grabbing onto a low branch, I began to climb, slinging one leg after the other over the limbs. High in the tree, I found a wonderful seat and ingested apple after apple. *What does my mom know?* I thought.

Well, I found out. I've never had such a stomachache—before or since.

Teenagers are a lot like green apples.

Parents want their adolescent to be mature. Ripened. We expect them to be ready in the summer. It seems autumn will never come.

Remember, as certainly as autumn replaces summer, maturation supplants immaturity.

School days, school days,
Dear ol' Golden Rule days,
Readin', 'n writin', 'n 'rithmetic
Taught to the tune of the hickory stick . . .

That song may represent an era of generations past, but as today's parents, we will someday look back on our children's school years as times that have brought warmth, laughter, delight, and wonderful memories to our home. A keepsake to forever cherish.

Coming to Grips

1. Look closely at yourself and ask, "How do I work with the school? If something is wrong, whom do I contact? Do I ever offer encouragement to faculty?"

2. Decide: "Whom do I need to contact at the school?" ________________ Write out what you want to say.
   ____
   ____

3. List at least one faculty member to whom you can write a note of thanks. ______________________

4. Find a pen, piece of paper (anything will do), envelope, and stamp. *Write the note*.

5. Briefly leaf through this chapter and decide on one area in which you need improvement. List it. ______
   ____
   ____

6. Write a brief outline plan of how you will carry it out.

7

Just Say "No"

Watching someone throw up makes me nauseous. Really sick. I thought I wasn't going to make it when Dan vomited a fifth of vodka into the wastebasket in the coach's office. Why they called me, I'll never know.

I looked closely at Dan. Long, dirty, greasy hair framed a face that looked much older than his years. His clothes were unkempt and they stunk. Alcohol and drugs had already taken their toll on this young man.

I listened to him sob out the gut-wrenching story of his pain. Liquor was the destructive way he chose to cope.

"Okay, so my kid got a little buzz on. Tipsy," one father expressed. "It's part of growing up. At least he's not on drugs." I've heard scores of similar comments from parents.

Alcohol is a *drug*—whether parents choose to admit it or not!

We are an alcohol-accepting society. Everyone drinks—or so it seems. Drinking at parties, during business deals, and at backyard barbecues is a sanctioned and normal part of most lifestyles. Even when someone gets drunk, most people excuse it:

"Well, she doesn't hold her liquor well."
"Everyone has gone overboard at one time or another."
"He's funny when he's had a little too much."

It's much harder to say, "He's/she's drunk." We tend to shy away from the hard truth.

As parents, we want to protect our children. So we pretend drinking or becoming intoxicated just isn't all that bad.

Sobering Facts about Alcohol Consumption

Studies indicate that a teenager can become a full-blown alcoholic *in only three months*. That's *ninety days!* Other studies show evidence it takes even less time. How frightening.

When we see someone who can really hold his or her liquor and drink everyone under the table, the person is often looked on as being a "real man or woman." Just the opposite is true. High tolerance of alcoholic beverages is one of the signs of *parent* alcoholism.

We think an alcoholic is the unshaven, bleary-eyed, dirty bum who shuffles through garbage in the gutters, carrying all of his belongings in a shriveled-up paper sack while swinging a bottle of booze in a filthy, leathery hand. In reality, most alcoholics only drink beer, and 95 percent of them are either employed or employable and are functioning members of society.

With horror, I remember the tragedy of two high school girls. In an unchaperoned neighborhood party where alcohol flowed, a group of boys challenged Amy and Christine to a drag race. At 2:00 A.M. the deafening sound of the car plummeting through a brick wall was heard for a quarter of a mile. Christine was driving, and she survived the accident. But she spent weeks in the hospital to heal physically, then months in a psychiatric ward for emotional trauma.

Her best friend, Amy, was buried—in her brand-new prom dress.

Alcohol removes inhibitions and greatly blurs the ability to make rational choices. Sometimes a teen indulges in liquor to dull emotional pain, but often it is done with friends just to have a good time. Disaster can be the result.

It has been reported that before high school graduation, 85 percent of all adolescents will experiment with alcohol. The Education Commission of the United States affirms that since 1960, drug and alcohol problems among adolescents have increased sixty times. We have a dilemma of epidemic proportions on our hands.

Causes of Alcoholism

In their book, *Drug Proof Your Kids,* Arterburn and Burns list some underlying reasons for the development of alcoholism:

- *Biological Predisposition*—The tendency toward alcoholism is inherited. In treatment centers, 50 percent are children of an alcoholic (usually the father). If both parents are alcoholics, the chances are even greater that the child will also become an alcoholic.
- *Peer Pressure*—Just saying "No" is not all that easy for teenagers (or for adults). We all want to be in

step, at least to some degree, with our peer group. Most of us do not want to be noticeably different from the pack.

- *Parental Attitudes*—Teenagers tend to go to greater lengths than their parents. They drive faster, take more chances, flirt with death, and drink more. So, if parents consume alcohol in the home, count on their kid drinking more. Very often, the teenager begins drinking from the home bar, where there is easy access. It's free.
- *Life Crises*—Liquor is used by multitudes as a coping mechanism. It alleviates the pain. Anesthetizes. Adolescents go for the bottle too.
- *Depression*—In a life crisis, booze is a way to escape depression. Negative coping.
- *Parenting Styles*—Parents have an obligation to be the ones who guide and discipline their children. When parents slip into the "buddy" role, their offspring are left without supervision and direction. It erodes their security.

Drugs—the Deadly Deception

Four male seniors in my high school spent Saturday morning in the park smoking marijuana, along with doing a variety of other drugs. By midafternoon, they decided to go for a ride. Piling into a car, they raced through town at high speeds, crossed a divided highway into oncoming traffic, and met their fate. Their bodies were hurled from the automobile. Two lay dead. One was hospitalized for months and has never regained the ability to think rationally. Only one escaped permanent injury, but had flashbacks of horror and lived with emotional pain and guilt.

The thought of our offspring taking drugs throws parents into a frightened, emotional tailspin. It's terrifying.

Even after having dealt with thousands of teenagers, it is still difficult for me to tell when a student is doing drugs. Because of their youth, they have great resilience. They bounce back extremely quickly and without adult detection.

Numerous times I've had kids say, "I can't believe my parents; I've been stoned out of my skull and they never catch on." I believe there are two reasons why parents aren't aware: (1) It's a terrifying thing to admit, and (2) the signs are often disguised.

Dr. Paul King, in his book, *Sex, Drugs & Rock 'n Roll*, lists fourteen signs of drug usage:

1. changes in patterns of behavior
2. decreased interest in school and schoolwork
3. increased irritability
4. doing things for excitement that rational people would call dangerous
5. disinterest in appearance
6. little motivation to perform tasks
7. valuables missing and unaccounted for (e.g., jewelry)
8. stealing outside the family
9. unexplained money, clothes, CDs, stereo equipment
10. change in taste, friends, music (for the worse)
11. preoccupation with the occult
12. physical problems (pale, red eyes; dilated pupils; slurred speech)
13. irrational, explosive episodes
14. parents who ignore the signs

In the above list, drug signs 1–6 look like normal adolescent behavior, but signs 7–13 would make most parents quite suspicious of drug use.

The key, as I see it, is *changes*—any kind. Look for unexplained differences in patterns of behavior, and do not try to rationalize them away.

Let's take a brief look at some of the more popular drugs.

Marijuana is cheap and accessible and twenty times stronger than plants harvested a decade ago. It is estimated 81 percent of teenage cigarette smokers will try pot.

When smoking marijuana, the senses are enhanced, but the ability to act on the sensations is gone. Both short-term memory and concentration are impaired.

Marijuana is the gateway to drug addiction.

Cocaine and crack are the most psychologically addicting of all drugs. They replace basic drives of hunger, thirst, and sex.

Cocaine is intensely euphoric, lasting ten to thirty minutes, followed by severe depression.

Crack is smoked and is euphoric in eight to ten seconds, lasting five to fifteen minutes. It is inexpensive.

Both drugs are readily available.

Inhalants ("Huffing")

"What did you sniff? We *know* you've been sniffing something. Tell me what it is—*now!*" The bleary-eyed student was totally unresponsive to the insistent queries of the policeman and administrators.

Trying a new tactic, I gently took her aside. "It's important that I tell the paramedics what you have inhaled. You are very dear to me, and I don't want you to die. Please tell me what you sniffed."

As tears coursed down her young, pretty face, the story came out. She, as well as other students, had been huffing fluorocarbon propellant from a spray can in the photography lab.

Inhaling is very popular—and dangerous. It can cause brain damage or death. It is highly euphoric and may bring about loss of control.

Common inhalants are correction fluid, airplane glue, nail polish remover, lighter fluid, hair spray, gasoline, butane, fabric protector—things that are labeled "May be harmful or dangerous to your health."

Paraphernalia to watch for include plastic bags, wet rags, or sacks.

Amphetamines (Speed)

Produced in the United States and extremely popular on the high school campus, speed can be purchased at low cost and is readily available. It is extremely addicting, and the death toll is increasing for those who are addicted.

In my private practice, I have had a number of adolescents hooked on the drug. To become free of their addiction, they have gone into an inpatient treatment center as well as extensive therapy upon release.

Current studies report 61 percent of adolescents will try drugs prior to high school graduation. The National Institute on Drug Abuse states the use of cocaine, crack, heroin, and LSD is rising and may soon rival the high rates of the 1970s.

I hope drugs are not here to stay. Sometimes I wonder.

Parental Denial

I've yet to hear a parent express gratitude that his or her kid is on drugs. Parents are paranoid about them. Terrified. The thought their child may be on drugs strikes fear deep into the hearts of adults. It's probably the main reason parents are so quick to deny the possibility their teen is using drugs.

Brent and Mark cut classes, failed courses, were discipline problems, and exhibited a don't-care attitude about life. A number of teachers suspected drug use and expressed their concern to me. I concurred.

Mr. Morgan was very concerned about his boys. He called the school on a consistent basis to check on attendance, grades, and so forth. In one of our many conferences, I bravely suggested, "Mr. Morgan, several teachers have spoken to me about the possibility of your sons using drugs. I have some suspicions as well and am very concerned."

The ordinarily respectful and polite Mr. Morgan went into a rage. Throwing up his arms and yelling, he bellowed, "All of you are just picking on my sons. I know them. They are *not* on drugs."

"I certainly hope they are not, Mr. Morgan," I returned. "I would encourage you, however, to take them to a clinic and get a urine sample, just to be certain."

His body shook as he screamed, "I will *never* take them for a urine test. My boys are *not* doing drugs." With that, he stormed out of my office.

Brent did not graduate. After graduation, I tried to talk with him about the courses he would need in adult school to become a summer grad. Frustrated, I said, "Brent, look at me. Listen to what I am saying." His glazed-over, bloodshot eyes were unable to focus, nor could his brain follow my instructions. How sad.

My advice is: If you suspect or if anyone suggests your child may be on drugs—*check it out*. Get a urine drug test. Hopefully, it will be negative. But at least you will know.

Heavy Metal Music

Dr. King, author of *Sex, Drugs & Rock 'n Roll*, cites a study that finds: "57 percent of chemically dependent youths prefer heavy metal music. 16.4 percent of non-drug users prefer heavy metal music." He continues, "The real problem [in heavy metal music] is the messages of hate, despair, Satan worship, suicide, deviant sex, and criminal behavior contained in the lyrics and acted out on stage."

"Look at this picture and accompanying story," a teacher said as she handed me an assignment her student completed. It was filled with drugs, killing, and death themes.

In talking to a variety of teachers in the English and social science departments, without exception they concurred that topics of violence, death, drugs, and satanism are not uncommon. "Five years ago," one teacher responded, "I would have been shocked to see what I now observe as commonplace."

Satanic and hard rock musical group T-shirts have been banned on our campus. I have noticed that the teenagers who smoke marijuana are usually heavy metal enthusiasts, and they have demonic symbols doodled all over their notebooks.

Jack Woolworth, teen counselor and originator of CARE Systems (Communication and Relationship Enrichment), suggests that the music to which an adolescent listens is directly related to his or her style of clothes, attitudes, and drug usage.

I hope that a word to the wise is sufficient.

Drug Proofing

Authors Arterburn and Burns *(Drug Proof Your Kids)* give seven ways in which parents can drug proof their teenager.

1. *Education*—Read, attend seminars, be informed. (Books are listed in the bibliography of this book for your consideration.)
2. *Prevention*—Reward responsible behavior; discipline alcohol and drug usage.
3. *Identification*—Watch for signs of abuse. Realistically and honestly evaluate the problem.
4. *Intervention*—Make it fast and appropriate.
5. *Treatment*—There are many treatment facilities. A few are listed later in this chapter.
6. *Supportive Follow-Up*—Get into a support group for parents and families. Become actively involved in your child's recovery program.
7. *Self-Evaluation*—Look closely and honestly into your drinking habits and prescription drug use. If you need help, do not delay. Solve your own addiction problem.

Adding to Arterburn and Burns's list, I believe there are additional ways to drug proof your teens:

Modeling is extremely important. Be honest with yourself, your teen, and others. Have a deep spiritual commitment to God—one that is life-changing and incorporated into every part of your daily life. Model traits of integrity and purity, and risk being truthfully vulnerable about your faults.

Fun is vital for a family's well-being. Plan good times together. It would be wonderful if fun occurred spontaneously, but usually a time must be set for it to happen. Laugh together. Life has painful and serious sides, but allow yourself to be frivolous once in a while. Be silly.

Previously, I briefly suggested obtaining a *urine sample*. If you suspect drug use, I encourage a urine sample from a drug treatment center so that it will not be contaminated by the teenager. These facilities are more alert to tampering possibilities.

The *eye check* is another excellent in-home drug check done with a pupilometer (small flashlight). This technique is used extensively by police departments and professional sports organizations to investigate and control drug use. An optometrist, ophthalmologist, or drug treatment center can give guidelines for an eye check at home. My optometrist states that pupilometers are available for purchase in most optometry offices, and the practitioners are usually happy to give instructions for their use.

Before you do the eye check, explain to your child that you will be checking his or her pupils periodically. State, "We are not examining your eyes because we believe you are taking drugs, but we want to help you to say 'no' when drugs are offered. You can tell your friends that your parents check your eyes for drug use; since you never know when it will occur, you can't take the chance of trying drugs. Place the blame on us. This is our way to help you remain strong."

I suggest you begin as early as ten years old, so your child will become accustomed to the check and will view it as a game. By the teenage years, it will be taken in stride.

Following are a few organizations that can be of help. The first three are Christian organizations.

1. Overcomers 1-800-310-3001
2. Teen Challenge 1-800-976-6990
3. New Life Treatment Center 1-800-227-LIFE
4. Narcotics Anonymous 818-780-3951
5. Alcoholics Anonymous 1-800-356-9996
6. Tough Love 1-800-333-1069
7. National Institute on Drug Abuse Hotline
   1-800-662-HELP (a national alcohol/drug treatment routing service)
8. Churches and Christian psychologists

Prayer is the greatest thing you can do for your teen. Present your child to God daily and ask for strength for your offspring to withstand peer pressure. Ask God for wisdom in raising your child. James 1:5 promises, "But if any of you lacks wisdom, let him ask of God, who gives to all men generously and without reproach, and it will be given him." This is surefire, folks.

I encourage you, as I did in chapter 1, to pray with your adolescent. When your teen is in bed, step into the room, tuck in the covers, and say a short prayer aloud. End with an "I love you" and a good-night kiss on the forehead. No matter how old, kids long for the tender touch and loving words of their parents.

Don't rescue. Let them take their lumps—the natural consequences of their behavior. This was previously detailed in chapter 4.

Instead of talking, *listen.* (See chapter 1 for a discussion of this important point.) Here's an encouraging statistic: 66 percent of *nondrug users* state their parents *listen* to them!

In Conclusion

Telling parents the truth about alcohol and drugs is difficult for me because I know it will produce fear and great anxiety. We all shudder to think the precious, innocent baby we once cradled in our loving arms could grow into an alcoholic or an addict.

If we follow the suggestions in this chapter, we have a much greater chance of never experiencing the gut-wrenching problem of addiction in our families. We must work as though everything depends on us, then pray as though everything depends on God. *He* is our hope.

Coming to Grips

1. Get in touch with your deep fears. Write down what scares you about possible alcohol and drug abuse in your teenager. ______________________________
____
____

2. On a scale of 1 (low) to 10 (high), score yourself in these areas:

   Family Fun
   1 2 3 4 5 6 7 8 9 10

   Modeling Values
   1 2 3 4 5 6 7 8 9 10

   Prayer for Your Child
   1 2 3 4 5 6 7 8 9 10

   Prayer with Your Child
   1 2 3 4 5 6 7 8 9 10

   Rescuing
   1 2 3 4 5 6 7 8 9 10

   Listening
   1 2 3 4 5 6 7 8 9 10

3. Name at least two of the above areas on which you will work.
   a. ____
   b. ____

4. Do you consume alcohol? _____ How much in a day? _____ in a week? _____ Do you take prescription drugs? _____ What kind? _______________ Number consumed daily? _____ weekly? _____ Do you need to cut back? _____

8

The Big "S" Word—Sex

We were standing in the middle of the supermarket. "Mommy," my preschooler said in a loud, clear voice. I knew that tone of voice and angelic expression. It meant a doozie was coming, one that meant I should be heading for the nearest exit—if I was smart. I wasn't.

"Where do babies come from?" she blurted. The normal din of a busy market suddenly became quiet. Every eye was on us—me, in particular. They were breathlessly waiting to hear how I was going to get out of this one.

"Well, Kathi," I whispered, "we'll talk about that later."

"Okay, Mommy," she again loudly responded. "But I wanna know . . ."

My heart dropped. *I may not be able to slip out of this one so easily*, I thought. A few people gave me a sinister half-grin.

"Can I see Mickey Mouse when we go to Disneyland?" my daughter finished.

"Yes, yes!" I almost screamed in relief.

When our kids are nearing or in the teenage years, we yearn for the earlier times when sex was no bigger deal than a visit to Walt Disney's Magic Kingdom.

But sex *is* a big deal to teenagers. I've spent hundreds of hours counseling adolescents about their sexuality, yet I strongly believe teens should be talking with their parents about sexual issues. Further, teenagers tell me they *want* to be able to talk with their parents. Surveys back it up.

Teenage Beliefs about Sex

Kids generally have a very different sexual belief system than adults. Here are a few examples:

"Virginity is not cool." Most boys (according to surveys) are relieved when they are no longer a virgin. Having their first sexual intercourse experience, in their thinking, is the rite of passage into adult masculinity. *Who* is not as important as *what*—the event.

Girls are more concerned about being "in love" with the boy to whom they relinquish their virginity. Females see it as an emotionally bonding experience.

Often both sexes are quite reluctant to admit in front of their peers that they are still a virgin. They are unwilling to suffer the cruel, negative comments that will ensue.

In his book *Why Wait?*, Josh McDowell asked fourteen- to sixteen-year-olds: "Have you engaged in sexual activities when you didn't want to?" Forty-seven percent of the boys and 65 percent of the girls answered "Yes."

There is great peer pressure.

"Sex in a relationship is okay." On the high school campus, there is an unwritten code that gives credence to sexual involvement within the context of a relationship.

"Give 'em condoms," scream the professionals. "They're already doing it. Teach them safe sex."

Garbage! No wonder kids don't abstain.

"Oral sex is not 'sex.'" If I had a buck for every time I've heard this comment, right now I'd be cruising down the open road in a brand-new, red Jaguar. Teens who claim virginity often admit to oral sexual encounters.

Penetration is the only thing most teenagers consider to be sex. It took me quite a while to internalize this concept. It was a hard one to believe.

Oral sex is widely practiced among adolescents. Because no pregnancy can occur, they feel safe. It never seems to dawn on them that there are such things as STDs (sexually transmitted diseases) and AIDS.

Outercourse is promoted by a variety of sex education curricula as well as politically correct organizations. In short, it means everything except penetration. How noble of these folks to teach our kids such debasing practices.

In working with teens, I adamantly claim that *any* type of sexual activity is sex, not just penetration. I'm always amazed at their looks of astonishment. My assertion, however, opens the door to talk in detail about sexuality.

Kids *want* to hear some straight talk from us.

"Using birth control is wrong." Multitudes of times I've heard, "If I take the pill or use birth control, it means I'm planning to do wrong. [Some even use the word *sin*.] I just can't do that. But, if sex just happens, it's forgivable."

Unfortunately, sex "just happens" about three times a week. Unprotected. Numerous girls who have told me this theory have done so with tears of shame, while experiencing extreme pain over their pregnancy.

College students say they're big on birth control, yet many don't use it. For the high schooler, it's practically nonexistent. Adolescents believe sex outside marriage is wrong, therefore, they don't take precaution by using birth control.

"Abortion is the only way out." In my state (California), an adolescent must have parental permission to have his or her ears pierced. Not so with abortion. As a high school counselor, I legally *cannot* inform the parent about an impending abortion but must protect the confidentiality of the student.

I always encourage the female student to tell her parents about the pregnancy and offer my services (at school) to the family. Some students tell their parents. Most do not.

The greatest concern of teenagers (even more than the pregnancy) is telling their parents. "It will kill them" is a frequent statement. Kids deeply love their parents and do not wish to bring pain and disappointment to them. To the traumatized teen, then, abortion seems the only solution. In my professional judgment, abortion is too easy, too accessible, and too affordable.

The Sexually Active Teenager

"Do you have a minute?" the trio asked. I could see an urgency on their somber, innocent-looking faces.

"Sure," I responded. "Come on in."

Lori, Alicia, and Courtney were all sophomores. About fifteen. I waited quietly for one of them to begin.

"We need some information," Courtey began. "Yeah, we're kinda scared," Lori continued. Alicia nodded in concurrence.

"We were wondering where we could get tested for AIDS?" gingerly came the words. "And we want to know about STDs," another chimed in.

"Sounds like you're worried," I commented. "Tell me what has been happening with all of you."

One by one their stories tumbled out. Lori was sexually active with her boyfriend, but he wasn't the one by whom she lost her virginity. Courtney had slept with a number of boys and was worried about AIDS and STDs. Alicia lost her virginity after last Friday's football game.

The National Center for Health Statistics as well as other organizations and surveys agree that by the time a student graduates from high school, over 80 percent of both boys and girls have lost their virginity and, of those, over 20 percent are sexually active.

As the trio's story began to unfold, I learned one particular boy had had sex with each of the girls, all the while he was involved in a steady relationship with another girl. They reported there were at least two more girls he was currently seducing.

"Let me draw you a diagram of how AIDS and STDs can spread," I proceeded. "I'll use circles. One circle represents you, and the other circle is your boyfriend.

"Let's say you've only slept with him. No one else. Your boyfriend, however, has had sex with three other girls."

"No way," they claimed in unison. "This guy has had at least six in the last few weeks."

"Alright, I'll draw him sleeping with six people."

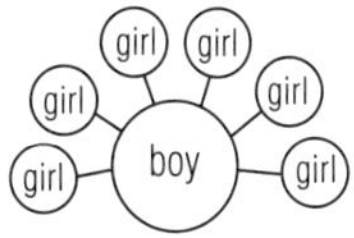

"Now, let's say each of these six people had sex with two more."

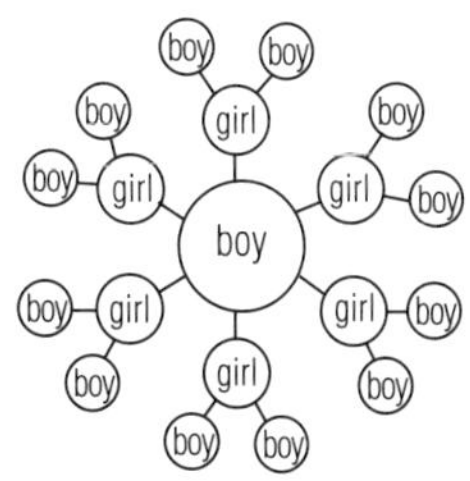

As I continued to draw circles and expand sexual partners, it was not hard to see how AIDS and STDs are becoming rampant. As I drew, the realization began to dawn on their shocked faces. The point hit home—hard.

When parents are absent (working), so is constraint. Other reasons for teen sexual involvement include:

need for love
desire for intimacy
want to be popular
wish to be macho
desire to be liberated
feeling obligated
want to prove love
wish to be an adult
curiosity
being in love
feeling lonely
peer pressure
rebellion

Alicia (the third part of the trio) came back the next day to talk about the loss of her virginity. Actually, she came to mourn. "I always thought Ray was so cute," she said. "I wondered what it would be like to be with him—or anyone. Yet my plan was to wait until marriage so it would be special."

Tears began to form in her dark brown eyes as she recalled the events. "I was feeling really lonely at the football game, and things weren't good at home either. My friends ran off, and I didn't know where they were. As the game ended, Ray came over to talk, and I was excited that he would pick me out, since he's a senior. He asked if I wanted to go for a Coke. Well, one thing led to another, and it happened." Tears began to splash all over her blouse.

Alicia returned to see me often. She needed a safe place to cry and grieve the loss of her virginity. Over and over she repeated one haunting phrase, "I gave up my virginity for a lousy Coke."

The Safe Sex Lie

Television, movies, talk shows, and psychologists have hooked us into believing that sex in an AIDS-filled world is safe. "Just use a condom," they advise.

Since the media has assured teens that condoms are safe, some adolescents choose to engage in "safe sex." They rationalize they can be loved (through sex), while having a safe, protected experience (through condom use).

However, most teens don't use condoms at all. Even with widespread information about the deadliness of AIDS and the accessibility of condoms, studies cite that few teenagers use a condom. One student body president was quoted in the school newspaper, "Condoms are good and should be used, but when the urge strikes—no one cares." How true.

Thus, safe sex is a big lie! Condom or no condom, *safe sex* is an oxymoron. One is safe from neither pregnancy nor AIDS.

The reason most married couples stopped using condoms years ago is because those condoms failed. Research has found the AIDS virus to be one thousand times smaller than the sperm. Additional medical studies state the AIDS virus may lie dormant for ten to fifteen years prior to a person becoming HIV positive.

A female is able to get pregnant only a few days out of each month, but a couple is susceptible to AIDS every day. That's safe sex? No way! Even if there occurs no pregnancy, venereal disease, or AIDS, a teen is not left unscathed.

Adolescents are looking for love, but when a teen becomes promiscuous, the opposite occurs. The emotionally wounded teenager will often be dumped and left with sadness, loneliness, and depression. Most teenagers wind up feeling used because sex does not fill the deep need to be loved. It seems like such an easy solution, but the aftermath of emotional trauma is deadly.

Pure Panic—Pregnancy!

I've seen the look scores of times. As a youthful girl slips into the chair on the opposite side of my desk, she is a picture of despair, dejection, and hopelessness. Her once sparkling eyes look dead—lifeless. Tears come in torrents as she sobs her inaudible story. Quietly I move toward the chair and encompass her head in my arms. With a death grip, she clutches me. It is as though I am the life preserver and she is drowning in a stormy sea of sorrow. Cries come from the depths of her soul; her body quivers and shakes under the pressure of insufferable pain.

I cannot begin to remember all their names over the years. They are legion. The scene is all too familiar.

Most pregnant girls I have counseled have had only one sexual experience. The younger they are, the more likely they will become impregnated during the first sexual intercourse.

Teens who bear children are less likely to complete high school, will have low paying jobs, 70 percent will be on welfare assistance, and 60 percent who marry the father will be divorced in five years. That's not a pretty picture.

Rarely does the father stick around. They are boys who are scared stiff. It is too much responsibility, too early, and they are too immature to cope with the consequences of their choices. Fleeing is their way out.

But the girl is left. Alone she must tell her parents, go through the pregnancy, bear the baby, and be confined for eighteen years in the role of raising a child.

Rarely have I seen the baby put up for adoption.

The "Easy" Road—Abortion

National Right to Life 1993 statistics state in the U.S.:

28 million abortions since 1973 (more deaths than all the U.S. wars combined)
4,300 abortions daily (1 every 20 seconds)
200,000 second/third trimester abortions yearly
93 percent of all abortions were used as birth control

Adolescent girls are terrified of telling their parents they are pregnant. Abortion seems to be the answer: It's cheap (free in many states), their friends recommend it as well as do most health care workers, and it's a secret.

The vast majority of pregnant teenagers I have encountered choose to abort. It is rare when a girl carries the baby to term.

"Mrs. Gordon, could I send Stacy in to see you immediately? Something is desperately wrong. She looks like she is going to pass out," Mr. Carson yelled into the phone.

I was aware Stacy had had an abortion the week before. A student accompanied her as she stumbled into my office. The blood had drained from her face, and I helped her into the chair as she drooped over my desk. "What's happening, Stacy?" I asked.

"I don't know," she responded. "I guess I'm in my period, but it's really bad. It keeps gushing."

She called the medical doctor at the abortion clinic from my office. When she described her symptoms, he merely said, "Well, get off your feet for a couple of days. You'll be okay."

If that doctor had been in my presence, he would have had bruises around his neck!

This is not an uncommon story. Abortion is a business—a big one. They are out for the bucks. Nothing more.

Not only do I have to deal with a sick kid, but later on the guilt sets in. Some push guilt aside, but it manages to crop up later. There are many women in my private practice who had abortions ten years ago and are just now experiencing tremendous guilt. I gently work through the process of healing and forgiveness with them.

Even though abortion is wrong (murder), we have a loving and forgiving God. Healing is possible.

Sexually Transmitted Diseases

Not a great deal is heard about STDs. People tend to think because gonorrhea and syphilis are relatively under control, everything is okay. Not so. In their book *Raising Them Chaste*, Richard and Renee Durfield state that two and one half million new cases of teenage STDs are reported each year. Here are a few more enlightening statistics from the Centers for Disease Control and U.S. Department of Health:

One in four sexually active teens will contract venereal disease before graduation from high school.

Adolescents (ages 10–19) and young adults (ages 20–24) are at a higher risk for acquiring STDs.

Sexually active adolescents have high rates of chlamydial infection.

Currently, chlamydia is exceeding the number of cases of gonorrhea in the United States. Both are often asymptomatic in women.

Rates of gonorrhea in women are particularly high in adolescents (highest among 15–19-year-olds).

Chlamydia has serious reproductive tract complications (pelvic inflammatory disease, infertility, and ectopic pregnancy).

Chancroid is a new health threat—3,500 new cases in 1991. Many go untreated because doctors mistake it for syphilis.

As parents, it's important to take a hard look at sexually transmitted diseases and to discuss it at great length with our adolescents.

The World Epidemic—AIDS

We hear so much about AIDS that we begin to turn off some of the information. As long as it doesn't touch our lives, we feel relatively safe.

In order to keep our awareness current, I will cite a few statistics from the Durfields' book, from Gene Antonio's *The AIDS Cover-Up?*, and from the U.S. Department of Health and Human Services for your consideration:

100 million worldwide are AIDS infected (10–15 million have died).

In the United States by the year 2000, 20 million will be infected with AIDS.

In New York, some hospitals have 50 percent AIDS patients at a medical care cost of $150,000 each.

AIDS is the seventh leading cause of death among fifteen- to twenty-four-year-olds.

It is estimated 21 percent of AIDS patients contracted the disease as teenagers (another study stated "nearly everybody").

(For further information, Gene Antonio's book, *The AIDS Cover-Up?*, is excellent and informative.)

My belief is that we cannot know too much about this dreaded disease. It must be a recurring and ongoing topic of conversation with our children.

AIDS will eventually affect all of us. In the last few years, two of my male friends have died of AIDS. With both men, we had ongoing spiritual talks. One stated, "I never knew what you meant by a *personal* relationship with Jesus Christ. Even though I grew up a religious person, I couldn't comprehend the difference. Now, I *know* what it is to be committed to Jesus, and my life is changed." I look forward to a huge bear hug when we meet in heaven!

Dating Age versus Sexual Involvement

I overheard an interesting conversation between a senior male and sophomore female student not long ago.

Boy: "So, who are you going to the prom with?"
Girl: "I'm not."
Boy: "A pretty girl like you. Why not? Haven't you been asked?"
Girl: "Yes, I've had several invitations, but I'm only fifteen. My parents won't let me date until I'm sixteen."
Boy: "That's dumb!"
Girl: "They only want what is best for me, and besides, I'll have chances later on when I'm old enough."

"Good for you," I chimed in. "I'm proud of you, and I totally agree with your parents. They are very wise. It's refreshing to know there are parents who care enough to set tough standards."

The senior boy looked at me like I had a screw loose.

In his book *Why Wait?*, Josh McDowell lists a very interesting and informative chart:

Age Began Dating	Percent Sex before Graduation
12	91%
13	56%
14	53%
15	40%
16	20%

Take this chart seriously. When kids begin dating early, there isn't much left to do by the time they're ready to graduate, other than to become sexually involved.

Abstinence—the Only Way to Go!

Many teens don't know what *abstinence* means, nor have they been encouraged to live a chaste lifestyle. We must encourage abstinence and talk about it straightforwardly.

Several years ago, Dr. Richard Durfield and I sat together at a conference—both of us unpublished writers. A couple of years later, he mailed me his first book, *Raising Them Chaste*—an incredible guidebook for parents.

Dr. Durfield has a concept called the "Key Talk" (once featured on *Focus on the Family*). It is an evening with the same-sex parent during which sex is discussed in great detail, ending with a signed covenant to remain chaste. Here is a sample of the evening:

1. A special restaurant meal together
2. Conversation that includes the value of sexuality and the importance of virginity until marriage

3. A question-and-answer time where nothing is off limits
4. Discussing the meaning of the covenant (a promise and agreement) of sexual abstinence until marriage
5. Prayer for your child's future spouse
6. Giving of an engraved key ring (signifies the key to his or her heart and sexuality) to be worn until marriage, at which time it is presented to the bride or bridegroom
7. Signing the covenant and sealing it with prayer

Dr. Rubin made a study of Christian adolescents who were active members at eight conservative, Christian, evangelical churches in the Midwest and South. Of those surveyed, 43 percent had had sexual intercourse by the age of eighteen, and an almost equal number had experimented with sexual behaviors that stopped short of intercourse.

If this is happening in our churches (which it is), as parents we cannot sit idly by. We're losing our kids!

The good news: the Southern Baptist Convention has developed an abstinence pledge program called "True Love Waits." It's sweeping the nation.

What's a Parent to Do?

Parents need to talk about sex with their kids—even though it's tough. Real tough. Teens *want* to talk and desire their parents' input and guidance.

Adolescents think about sex all the time. One survey states boys think about it every eighteen seconds. So you needn't worry you will be bringing up a foreign subject.

One approach is when your children view a television program or movie, explore the moral values. Ask them what they think. Tell them your views—and why.

Talk about some of the major reasons for getting into sex. (You can start with the list on page 118.) Examine the ramifications of sexual involvement and the rewards of abstinence.

Open up the topic of sex with both your boy and girl (no double standards). One study stated that of 1,400 parents, only 15 percent of mothers and 8 percent of fathers discussed sex with their children. Explain the law of diminishing return—that which satisfied us today demands more tomorrow. It escalates.

Dr. James Dobson gave a sexual progression in his book *Love for a Lifetime*. It serves as a guideline in setting sexual limits:

Eye to body—noticing another person, being attracted

Eye to eye—both persons see each other at the same time

Voice to voice—begins with a short conversation

Hand to hand—touching and holding, mostly nonromantic

Hand to shoulder—an arm around the shoulder of a friend

Hand to waist—signifies romance is intended

Face to face—kissing and caressing

Hand to head—becomes more familiar (running fingers through a person's hair); in our culture we do not touch the heads of other people unless we are intimate (or getting a haircut)

Hand to body—more intimate body examination

Mouth to breast

Touching below the waist—sexual exploration

Intercourse

At any level, a line can be drawn—one that will not be crossed. The farther a person progresses, the more difficult it is to abstain from intercourse. Dr. Dobson suggests that the last four steps are for marriage. I agree.

With your child, concentrate on the beauty of waiting until the wedding night to be sexually involved. I heard it explained this way: Sex is the healing balm that carries newlyweds over the rough places. Whenever sex is shared with anyone else before marriage, a little bit of the balm is used up in each encounter, thus leaving only a fraction (if any) balm available for the tough times in marriage. It was indiscriminately given away—wasted.

Working with couples in therapy, I see a lot of pain stemming from having had previous sexual partners. There is blaming and a great deal of mistrust. It *never* makes for a better marriage.

A teacher used a rose to create a powerful illustration. She told the boys in the class, "This rose represents a girl. Each time you have sex with her, you're taking a nonreplaceable part of her." Then she asked each boy in the class to take one petal. To the last boy, she gave the bare rose stem and said, "This is your wife."

Look again very closely at Josh McDowell's chart comparing early dating with sexual involvement (see page 125) and make some hard decisions regarding dating practices for your teenager. Share the chart with your child and talk about the logical consequences of early dating.

Emphasize with your adolescent the human need to be intimate (have someone know us totally yet love us completely). Talk about the natural desire to have intimacy in marriage—ability to be real, vulnerable, honest, relaxed. Point out that sexual involvement outside of marriage will destroy or greatly damage the steps toward intimacy.

When people meet, there is an attraction level. As the relationship progresses, there are many steps that must be taken prior to intimacy. Sexual involvement cuts the process short, and intimacy may never be achieved. Thus, one of our greatest needs will go unfulfilled.

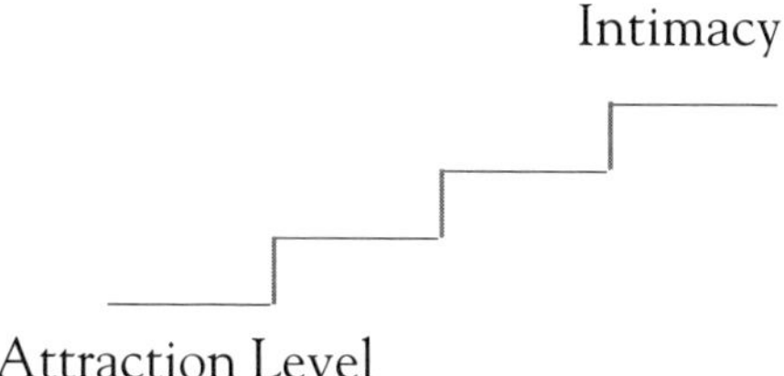

As I have held weeping, pregnant girls in my arms and empathized with them in their excruciating pain, I believe God sees the same picture. That's why he commands sexual abstinence outside of marriage—not to ruin our life or demand we miss out on the fun, but he wants us to *miss out on the pain*. In his love, he says "No." He desires for us a life full of excitement, intimacy, and health.

Maybe you're a parent whose child has crossed the sexual line, perhaps into pregnancy or abortion. It's vital to separate the act from the person. Good people do wrong things—all the time. That does not make your child a totally bad person, rather, just one who has done a wrong deed. Keep the two separate.

The good news is there is healing, forgiveness, and hope. There is such a thing as "secondary virginity" (commitment to no further sexual involvement prior to marriage)—a new beginning.

Finally, get involved in the sex education programs at your school. A good friend of mine was very concerned about her two teenage daughters and the sex education curriculum. She fought the system by skillfully, kindly, and firmly presenting her reasons to the principal for an abstinence-based education. Not only was such a program approved for the school, but they had an assembly on date rape. It can be done!

Two such abstinence-based curriculums are: *Pro-Chaste*, P.O. Box 5, Solano Beach, CA 92075-0005, and *Sex Respect: The Option of True Sexual Freedom, A Public Health Guide for Parents*, by Coleen Kelly Mast, 1986. The *Sex Respect* program is in all fifty states and twenty-six countries, involving eighteen hundred school districts (as of 1992).

Some suggestions to get started:

1. Call your junior high or high school to find out what sex education program is being used.
2. Get in touch with the school district office to see if there are abstinence programs available.
3. If abstinence-based curriculum is available but not being used, or if it is not accessible, get a few parents together to attend a school board meeting and speak to the issue. Do your homework. Be knowledgeable, concise, kind, yet firm. Keep slowly plugging away until change occurs.

In Conclusion

The topic of sexual issues is of great concern to parents. Most of us have sweaty palms and a palpitating heart when we think about talking to our kids. Yet it's just one of those tough parenting jobs that *must* be done.

I wish I could honestly tell you I did a wonderful job of discussing sex with my daughter. I didn't. Not only was I a super wimp, my self-esteem was low, my marriage was dysfunctional, and I had no idea how to approach the subject or what to say. So I handed her a book—one that was of little help. I guess I felt I had done my parenting job. Nothing could be further from the truth.

Fortunately, I've learned. I'm no longer the unhealthy person of years ago. Not only do I pass on my expertise of working with thousands of teenagers and parents, my therapeutic training, and my insight, but my advice comes from a parent's heart who knows how tough it is.

So I encourage you to travel a difficult road—talk to your teenager about sex. It's a path with lasting rewards.

Coming to Grips

1. Reread the section "Teenage Beliefs about Sex." Are there areas that surprised you? Angered you? Scared you? List them. ______________________________
____
____

2. What is your greatest concern for your child in the sexual area? ______________________________
____
____

3. Write down your plan to talk very honestly and openly with your teen about sex.
   a. ______________________________
   ____
   b. ______________________________
   ____
   c. ______________________________
   ____
   d. ______________________________
   ____

4. Check out the sex education curriculum of your school by following these steps:

   a. Name a few supportive friends________________
   ____
   ____
   ____

   b. Write or call to obtain information about an abstinence-based curriculum.

   c. Identify the school official with whom you should talk (large school, a counselor; small school, an assistant principal or principal).
   Name ____________________ Phone ______________

   d. Call the board of education district office to see when they meet (day and time), and ask for a spot on the agenda to present your case.
   Phone ______________
   Directions you were given:____________________
   ____
   ____

The Hidden Crime—Date Rape

It was one of those normal kind of work days. Late in the afternoon I had a surprise visit from a former high school grad.

She looks so fresh and young—so pretty, I thought. Her hair was pulled back in a French braid, and she looked adorable. However, the expression on her face did not match. I knew something was terribly wrong. There was a huge knot in the pit of my stomach, and my heart sank as I listened to her painful tale.

A number of years have elapsed, and I asked her if she would be willing to write her story. These are her words:

> We met our freshman year of college during orientation, and we discovered his family and my father were close friends.

By the time we were twenty, Dennis (not his real name) and I were best friends. He left college for a military career. As friends, we spent a lot of time together, even though he was in a serious relationship with someone else. I had made it my personal mission to break down the towering walls of his protected personality. I had no romantic feelings for him, but I felt I could meet his needs.

I invited him over to my mom's house for dinner one night. I thought we could have a leisurely meal, play a game, and then go back to the dorm. I knew that no one would be home that weekend, but I saw no danger, as I trusted Dennis implicitly.

Upon arrival at the house, Dennis reached into the glove compartment and pulled out a gun—a .357 magnum. When I reacted in alarm, Dennis just laughed and made me feel stupid.

Later, out of the blue, he asked me if I had ever been raped.

"You know I haven't. Why would you ask me that?" I replied with a strange sense of alarm.

"Well, you're so afraid of sex," he said.

"You know how I feel about sex, Dennis!" I was a virgin and had committed to stay that way until marriage.

He suddenly picked me up.

"What are you doing? Put me down," I laughed.

In the time it took to be carried from one end of the hall to the other, I had gone from laughter to stark terror. I watched Dennis's face change to a demonic evil. I remember grabbing at doorjambs along the way and kicking and screaming. As he threw me on the bed, I knew my screams would never be heard.

During the rape, I glanced at the end of the bed. A sense of peace flooded me as I saw Jesus Christ standing there. He said, "I will never leave you nor forsake you." I knew I had been allowed the experience of meeting Christ face-to-face in the midst of the most terrifying moment of my life.

I went back to the dorm and sat in the shower with the water running for four hours. Crying.

The next day I told my close friend, but she said I was making too big a deal out of it.

It took me two weeks to see a doctor and gather the courage to go to the police. I felt tremendous guilt and responsibility for allowing myself to be in such a vulnerable situation, but I wasn't able to press charges because most rapists are set free and the victim is the one on trial.

I shared my experience in a group counseling situation. The therapist (a doctoral student) said, "I'm so glad you shared about the rape. Now I have some material for my term paper."

A few weeks later, I went to a trusted professor at my Christian college who also knew Dennis. Tearfully, I poured out my story. Finally my professor replied, "You must be mistaken. That's not the Dennis I know."

I experienced four months of sleeplessness, depression, and constant vomiting, with no menstrual cycle, and became fearful I was pregnant. My doctor refused to do a pregnancy test ("You can't get pregnant from a rape"), and home tests did not yet exist. I knew I couldn't have an abortion, so I decided to leave school when the pregnancy became evident, then raise the child on my own, with some help from my family.

After four months, I finally started my period, and the other physical manifestations of the rape lessened. I realized that financially I would not be able to obtain any further psychological help.

It has taken years to work through the emotional and psychological results of the rape. The memories will forever bring back pain, but I have finally come to the point of forgiving Dennis for his brutality.

Jesus Christ has been my Counselor. He has helped me to see areas where the rape is still affecting me and gently, often with more tears and pain, helps me to give those areas over to him.

> I urge victims of date rape to seek counseling. Also, allow Jesus to bear the pain and bring health and restoration.

The victim is Kathi, my daughter. This was her journey of pain—and mine.

After she poured out her story that afternoon in my office, I took Kathi immediately to the police. She was unable, however, to file charges for fear of ruining Dennis's military career.

My emotions were many. I desperately wanted to kill Dennis. I truly believe I would have had no problem taking his life. The anger and rage were more venomous than any I have experienced before or since.

I didn't know what to do. Fear gripped me at every turn. Was Kathi pregnant? Would we have a baby to raise? The physician kindly told me, "I cannot talk to you about your daughter's medical condition [he didn't use the word *rape*] because she is legally an adult."

Kathi asked me to keep the rape confidential. Because I chose to support her desire, my personal resources were nil.

My deep desire was to be there for Kathi. I thought I was, but as I take a truthful look back, it was not to the extent she needed. As the weeks wore on, we didn't talk about it much, and I erroneously (probably with relief) assumed she was doing okay, having no idea of the painful rejections she suffered from the people to whom she reached for help.

My memory seems to indicate I offered professional help, but she was unwilling. If that is the case, Kathi now believes her refusal was based on the excruciating spurning she received from her professor and the counselor intern. She could not risk that again.

For me, the writing of this chapter has been one of abundant tears, great pain, overwhelming emotions, and an aching heart. Regrets. "If only I had . . . ," "Why didn't I . . . ?" Questions for which there are no answers. If there were any way I could possibly turn back the clock and do differently———. There isn't. I am willing, though, to be completely honest with Kathi, myself, and God and to forgive myself for being emotionally unable to be the mother I would like to have been.

Yet the most precious part of Kathi's story (which I learned only recently) was when Jesus stood by her bedside during the most traumatic, desperate time of her life. I must leave my pain with him, as did Kathi, because he truly understands.

On my bedroom wall hang the wooden letters, *P T L*. They stand for "Praise the Lord." One tearful morning several months following the rape, I arose from a torturous and fitful night. As I looked at the letters, God's gentle whisper changed them to read *"Peace through the Lord."* I was confident he would get us through. He did!

A Realistic Look at Date Rape

In the ensuing years, I have counseled numerous rape victims. Looking through the eyes of a therapist, I have picked out several things in Kathi's story that are common (or at least red flags) in victims.

As a parent, I strongly suggest you look for specific signs in your daughter that suggest she may be a potential rape victim. Discuss the issues with her beforehand and stay aware.

1. Kathi stated, "I felt I could meet his needs." It seems there was a feeling of being overly responsible for Dennis's mental health. She even used one phrase, "my personal mission." Victims tend to feel a great obligation for the welfare of others, rather than themselves. Their wishes, feelings, and needs are kept on the back burner as they desperately try to be all things to an unhealthy person. They tend to be rescuers.

2. The perpetrator was "trusted implicitly." Trusting an emotionally unhealthy person without any reservations is asking for big trouble. Offenders tend to be unpredictable, unstable, and capable of greatly damaging another human being. Caution is the key. Not trust.
3. Dennis pulled out a gun, then made light of the shock he caused. Kathi commented, "Dennis just laughed and made me feel stupid." An unhealthy person generally turns around his own dysfunction and gets the victim to believe it is her problem. As long as the victim thinks she is the one who is at fault, the perpetrator remains in control and can easily manipulate however he chooses.
4. Dennis suggested Kathi had a sexual problem because she had chosen to remain a virgin until marriage. He also used the word *rape*, which would frighten most young women. With each step, he was coming closer to his plan. Yes, plan! Rapes are usually not spur-of-the-moment events. They are often thought out or at the least fantasized prior to execution.
5. In date rape, the victim is often too embarrassed to scream, fight, or truly believe her "friend" could hurt her—until it's too late. It reminds me of a cat and mouse. The cat continues to bat around the mouse, and the mouse is hoping some miracle will happen. But it doesn't, and he is eaten.

   The victim (Kathi) could not bring herself to believe a rape would occur. But criminals mean business!

The Aftermath

Keep it a secret, most rape victims think. Somehow they get the irrational idea it was their fault. Often they believe it was deserved. They had it coming. Untrue! (Unfortunately, the self-blame often comes from the reaction of friends or others the victim turns to for support.)

The body enters a state of shock. (The medical doctor stated the rape was so violent that Kathi's internal organs were moved out of position.) The mind is irrational; the thinking process is incoherent or nonexistent. Confusion. Denial. Date rape victims have been known to have a normal conversation and a cup of coffee with the malefactor following the rape.

"I feel so dirty" is a statement I've heard many times. Kathi sat under the shower crying for four hours—quite normal for rape victims. They desperately and unsuccessfully try to wash away the emotional filth and pain they are experiencing. The common act of showering also destroys evidence needed in a court of law.

Kathi experienced additional, unbearable pain when she entrusted her dreaded secret to friends, a Christian professor, psychologist intern, and family doctor. In no way can anyone know the depths of despair, terror, and trauma a rape victim has undergone unless they, too, have been raped. So it's easier to brush the victim aside. Not deal with it. Pretend. Probably because they feel helpless.

A few months ago, one of my date rape patients decided to take her case to court. A virgin before she was violated, she now has herpes. But our court system revictimizes the victim. The emotional and financial cost was too much. She gave up.

Society and Date Rape

My strong concern is that the main reason rape victims remain silent is because our society does not see date rape as a crime. Many people believe "they asked for it."

How tragic!

Date rape is on the rise largely because of the current belief system. At a Rhode Island rape crisis center, 1,700 junior high students responded to the following questions:

"Is it okay to force a woman to have sex if the man has spent money on her?"
25 percent of the boys and 16 percent of the girls answered *yes*
"Is it okay to force a woman to have sex if they have dated six months?"
65 percent of the boys and 47 percent of the girls answered *yes*

This report exposes the thoughts of kids who are barely into adolescence. No wonder date rape is rampant. The guys tend to feel sex is their just due, and girls tend to go along.

As parents, we cannot change the American viewpoint. However, we *can* teach our daughters to protect themselves and our sons to know and stay within the guidelines of female respect.

It Can Happen to You is an incredible little book on date rape by Josh McDowell. Here are his guidelines for girls:

1. Set your limits and communicate them.
2. Avoid men who exhibit male myth characteristics (female disrespect of *any* kind).
3. Learn to say "no" and mean it.
4. Avoid excessive amounts of one-on-one time.
5. Be aware/suspect of unintentional messages.
6. Say "no" to alcohol and drugs.
7. Avoid blind dates.
8. Trust your instincts.
9. Use wisdom and common sense.

His advice for the males:

1. Realize that it is never okay to force a girl to have sex.
2. Stop what you're doing when she says "no."

3. Avoid the stereotype of the dominant, aggressive male.
4. Keep your eyes from wandering.

Excellent advice!

I would earnestly suggest you take your daughter or son out for dinner and have a heart-to-heart talk about the issues of date rape. Since it's such a delicate subject, you may want to read this chapter aloud to your child as a springboard for the discussion.

Insure against date rape entering your home. Envision this plan as a free insurance policy—with wonderful dividends. Use it!

P.S. I have forgiven Dennis, but it still hurts sometimes.

Coming to Grips

1. Write a paragraph on your fears, after reading this chapter: ______________________________

____
____
____
____
____
____
____

2. Write out a simple plan to talk with your daughter. List things you wish to discuss:
   a. ______________________________
   b. ______________________________
   c. ______________________________
   d. ______________________________
   e. ______________________________

3. Now write out a similar plan for the discussion with your son:
    a. ______________________________
    b. ______________________________
    c. ______________________________
    d. ______________________________
    e. ______________________________

4. List five things you would do if your child were date raped:
    a. ______________________________
    b. ______________________________
    c. ______________________________
    d. ______________________________
    e. ______________________________

Suicide—the Only Way Out?

As I sit here alone in the world
I constantly think of death
My body has been invaded
A shock that took my breath
My mind is in confusion
I don't know what to think
Tomorrow my life could be over
It could happen in a blink
I think of what had happened
Of what he did to me
All I ever want now
Is to have my soul set free
I feel like the fault [is mine]
No matter what they say
I know I'll never escape the pain
I relive it every day
I feel like I've done wrong

All I can do now is cry
As I look up one more time
And kiss the world good-bye

Cynthia
(used by permission)

Cynthia (not her real name) was fifteen years old when these painful lines were penned. She had been raped by a neighborhood boy, and the emotional trauma was excruciating. Her parents were divorced, and her mom didn't want her, so her dad had custody. Hopelessness filled her life. It took many hours of therapeutic intervention with Cynthia before healing began to emerge.

Suicidal thoughts or feelings among adolescents are not unusual. It is impossible to remember all the names, faces, or stories of the many students I have counseled through suicidal ideation.

One study says that 10 percent of high school students think about suicide; my experience indicates it is much higher. I believe *most* students, at one time or another, entertain suicidal musings.

Here are a few facts on suicide compiled from a variety of studies:

- Suicide is currently a leading cause of death among the young.
- In the under twenty-five age group, suicide has increased 130 percent in the past fifteen years.
- Female nonvirgins are sixteen times more prone to suicide.
- At the time of suicide, one-third had been drinking.
- Girls attempt—boys complete. (Girls take pills or slash wrists, while boys hang themselves, use guns, or drive their car into something.)

The Sad Persons Scale was developed by W. M. Patterson, H. A. Dohn, J. Bird, and G. A. Patterson to evaluate hospitalized suicidal patients. They came up with a composite of a suicidal person:

above thirteen years
depressed
previous attempt
alcohol abuse
rational thinking loss
social supports lacking (family, religion)
organized plan
no spouse or close primary relationship
sickness (chronic, debilitating, severe)

Most suicidal persons give a lot of thought to their suicide plan, and they also give clues to those around them. Here are some warning signs:

prevailing sadness
lack of energy
difficulty concentrating
loss of interest or pleasure in usual activities
atypical acting-out behavior
alcohol/drug abuse
sexual promiscuity
sudden or increased activity
drop in grades
social isolation
disruption in family (divorce/separation, especially the same-sex parent)
recent death or suicide attempt of loved one

change in eating or sleeping patterns
verbal remarks about sense of worthlessness, failure, death
preoccupation with death and violence
hoarding of pills, knives, ropes, etc.
attempts to put personal affairs in order
previous suicide attempts
proneness to accidents
disregard for personal appearance
truancy

Getting Help—Fast

Always take a suicidal statement seriously.

Often a teacher sends a student who has expressed a death wish (verbally or in writing) to see me. Other teenagers have come to me in agony because they are worried about a friend's possible suicide.

In counseling suicidal people, I confront the suicidal issue head-on.

"Jaime, I asked you to see me because I'm very concerned about you," I explained. "In fact, several of your teachers or friends have talked to me about you.

"We have noticed some drastic changes that scare us. You seem very depressed, like life just isn't worth it. Jaime, have you ever thought about suicide?"

Her head nodded, as her downcast eyes filled with tears and dribbled onto her slumped torso.

I waited. The tears continued to slip down her pale cheeks.

"Do you have a plan, Jaime?" I softly inquired.

There was an almost inaudible "yes."

"Tell me what it is, Jaime," I gently prodded.

"Pills, I guess," she whispered.

"What kind of pills?" I responded.

"Oh, just whatever," she mumbled.

"Tell me what is so painful," I continued. "I see great suffering in your eyes."

Jaime went into a story of great anguish, recounting the traumatizing events in her life.

"Jaime," I proceeded, "let's say you commit suicide. Then what?"

"I dunno. Guess it's just all over," she answered.

"But, what if it isn't? What if there is life after death?" I commented.

At this point, a bit of reality usually sets in. Most kids believe there could be some sort of heaven or hell and begin to talk about it.

As a Christian, I feel it is my obligation to bring up the spiritual issue. This is the one time in therapeutic settings where I address life-after-death issues *before* the client chooses to do so. Numerous times I have agonized over a teenager who has committed suicide and wondered, "Did my life mean anything to this kid? In the last moments of life, did he or she reach out to Jesus because of our conversations?" Therefore, I must confront a teen (or adult) with the hereafter and a simple, straightforward message of salvation.

We then talk in great detail about the path of pain their parents, siblings, family, and friends will travel because of their rash deed.

Here are a few suggestions:

1. As parents, verbalize concern for your child. If he or she cannot talk openly with you, find someone (a family member, pastor, friend, therapist, suicide hotline) with whom your teen can be honest.

2. Do *not* leave the adolescent alone.
3. If there is medication in the house, confiscate it. The same goes for guns, knives, and even car keys. (Many young men use an automobile as a device of death.)

Then, get professional help—*fast!* Suicide can be averted. Fortunately there *is* another way out, and therein lies the hope.

Coming to Grips

1. Look at the twenty-one warning signs of suicide on pages 145–46. Check off any that apply to your teenager.

2. Now rank them according to possible danger. For instance, if there is a gun in the house, rank it at the top.

3. Think through a plan you could follow if needed.
   Name of friend to call ______________________
   Telephone number ______________________
   Name of a therapist (highly recommended) ________
   ____
   Telephone number ______________________
   Medications/implements to confiscate ___________
   ____

4. Write out a short paragraph you can say to your child that will: (a) express great love and concern, and (b) confront your suspicions. ________________
   ____
   ____

5. If your teen has a suicide plan (of any kind) in mind, get professional help immediately!

Keeping Your Teen's Self-Confidence out of the Toilet

The only way we can get this world back on track, is to go back to the basics: how we raise our kids.

Lee Iacocca

Wise advice.

Most of us do not only want to get our kids grown and out of the house, we also want them to be productive, good citizens, possess a strong commitment to the Lord, and feel good about themselves—self-respect. The World Book Dictionary defines self-respect as: "Respect for oneself; proper regard for the integrity of one's character, or position with recognition of its obligations for worthy conduct." It describes self-esteem as:

"The thinking well of oneself; self-respect. The thinking too well of oneself; self-conceit."

God's Word also has some things to say about self-esteem: "As he thinks within himself, so he is" (Prov. 23:7).

Psychologists are now saying that the thoughts we allow to germinate in our minds today will determine who we will become in five years. Scripture stated the concept thousands of years ago: "I say to every man among you not to think more highly of himself than he ought to think; but to think so as to have sound judgment" (Rom. 12:3). It does not condemn thinking well of ourselves but warns us about crossing the line into arrogance. God wants us to have an *honest and accurate* evaluation of who we are—strong points and weak areas.

Concentrating on the Strengths

Many of us concentrate on our weaknesses rather than our strengths. For instance, take criticism. If we hear one negative comment, what do we usually do? Obsess. Constantly we roll it over and over in our minds and dwell on it. The more frequent, positive remarks often take a backseat.

One important way we can help our adolescent become stronger in his or her positive regard is to watch how we say things. Avoid using all-inclusive words such as *never*, *always*, *all*—condemning/negative words. None of us will thrive and produce under a person who is constantly on our backs. We will either retreat into our shell of conformity or come out with our dukes up ready to go a few rounds.

When your child is down on himself or herself, sit down together and write out his or her positive traits. Then discuss each one. Teens tend not to be aware of the good things we see in them.

In my high school, we have a student study team. It consists of the student, his or her parent, counselor, teachers, and an administrator. I often call the half-hour meeting because the adolescent is failing most classes, cutting school, and has discipline problems.

We begin the meeting by each adult stating the positive attributes of the student and writing them on the board. Often, this will bring tears to the eyes of a hardened teenager as he or she hears himself or herself described with kindness and honesty—especially from parents. My guess is this young person has heard mostly negative comments from his or her elders, or perhaps the positive statements never got through.

So take time in the discussion with your teenager to talk about all of his or her virtuous traits. Look at such things as physical appearance, personality, helpfulness, smile, friendliness, talents (musical, artistic, sports, mechanical), courage, doing a job or chore well (you may have to stretch for this one). Get creative. Verbalize appreciation for your child.

Help your teen to set *realistic* goals—stretching but attainable. Make sure the goals are in your child's area of strengths so he or she can experience the satisfaction of achievement.

Compensation

As a timer of track events, I remember the first time I saw Johnny run. He was a sight to behold. He reminded me of an old, wrecked car that was out of line. As each foot awkwardly crossed over the other, I was positive he would fall flat on his face. All the while his arms were flailing wildly. At first it was a comical sight. Then I gazed with my heart.

Johnny was a young man who was greatly handicapped. He also walked just like he ran—spastically. Over the next three years, the more I observed Johnny's bizarre maneuvers around the track, the more my admiration grew. Whether Johnny finished first or dead last, he had learned to compensate for his physical impairment and courageously struggled against the odds.

Help your adolescent learn ways to compensate for his or her weaknesses. Encourage him or her to try new things: volunteering in the community, baking, working on cars, involvement in church youth groups and school activities, sports, band, yearbook, newspaper staff, musical groups, service clubs. Help your teen find his or her niche.

Then there was Clarence. As the June sun was fading into the brilliant red-orange sky, tears came to my eyes as I watched Clarence. He was the last senior of nearly five hundred students to come on stage to receive his just due—graduation.

Not unlike Johnny, Clarence laboriously floundered up the stairs to the stage and with lurching body and outstretched hand, received his diploma. Then, with a broad grin traversing his grimaced face, his body clumsily maneuvered down the aisle toward his seat. As though on cue, the entire senior class rose to their feet, wildly screaming and applauding a classmate for whom they had great respect.

Most teens do not have the limiting handicaps of Johnny and Clarence. But they do have handicaps. As parents, it is our joy and responsibility to help our children compensate and cope in a world that is not always so accepting.

Setting Appropriate Boundaries

Healthy boundaries hold in the good and keep out the bad.

As adults, we usually remember the school bully. We also recall the times we were inadvertently or deliberately hurt emotionally by another person. Dr. James Dobson states in his book *Hide or Seek*, "School is a dangerous place for children with fragile egos."

As parents, we have a duty to prepare our kids for survival on the school campus as best we can, by teaching them to set solid boundaries for themselves and others.

I believe the fundamental boundary is respect—for themselves, fellow students, and adults. Children learn respect when it is required at home among family members.

In my experience, the vast majority of students are extremely respectful to me—even when I must mete out discipline. Rarely do I have a student who is impudent. I believe the parents have instilled a sense of respect for authority in their teen.

It is vital for me (and the parents) to respect the student by listening, thereby honoring the student's feelings, thoughts, and statements. Once a student is allowed to express his or her concerns, he or she is usually quite willing to do what is needed or asked by the adult.

Sometimes, parents disrespect their children. I've heard parents discuss their teens' faults in front of them—as if the teens were invisible. Most students sit through it with a look of shame and embarrassment. Others have turned it off years ago—on the outside. Inside those teens are raw and bleeding.

This is not to say parents should never discuss their concerns with a professional, family member, or friend. However, it needs to be done in private.

Overprotection can also be a form of disrespect, because the child has not been given adequate training or encouragement to handle difficult situations.

Whenever a screaming, wild-eyed parent comes into my office, I can count on the child to be passive, wimpy, and totally unable to protect or stand up for himself or herself. The adolescent has learned that not only will the parent aggressively fight the child's battles, but the parent believes his or her child to be *incapable* of presenting his or her own needs and desires. This teen's self-confidence is in the toilet. If you want your children to have little to no interpersonal survival skills, then make sure you constantly rescue them, manipulate others to meet their needs, and allow them no room to deal with people and problems on their own.

One mother of five nearly drove me crazy until all her kids graduated. All of her children were really fine young people, but they were so protected that they were unable to fend for themselves emotionally. I recently ran into her eldest in the community. He had completed college, was twenty-seven years old, and was engaged to be married. Even with his intelligence, hard work, and fine values, he exuded poor self-esteem, intimidation, and uncertainty. How sad.

Jay Kesler, author of *Ten Mistakes Parents Make with Teenagers*, suggests parents need to respect their teens' opinions, property, and privacy. We've discussed listening to the opinions, so let's look at respecting their property and privacy.

"Hey, when my daughter has a girlfriend in her bedroom, I crack the door and listen. I also constantly go into the room to 'get something.' When she is at school, I rummage through her drawers and notebook to see what's going on," one parent expressed.

This is not an isolated case. I hear it all the time.

I don't know about you, but I would be furious if my personal mail were read or my journal of intimate thoughts and prayers to God were scrutinized. When teenagers find their parents have been snooping around, not only are they enraged, but they also feel invaded and violated. Frankly, they have been.

I received a frantic call from a parent: "A note fell from my daughter's notebook, and I read it. It sounds like she wants to commit suicide. What should I do?"

"First, be honest about reading the note," was my reply. "Then talk to your daughter about your great love and concern, and let her know you will get professional help for her immediately."

If you read or find personal things, admit it. Then confront the issue in kindness, concern, and love.

By setting boundaries of respect for yourself and others, there is a good chance your teenager will follow suit.

Being an Encourager

Several years ago I was in a group where wonderful things were said about Chuck Swindoll (*Insight for Living* radio speaker and former pastor of First Evangelical Free Church of Fullerton, California). As is my custom, I wrote him a letter.

"I need to tell you what people are saying behind your back," was my tongue-in-cheek beginning. Then, I passed on the compliments verbatim.

In reply, he wrote, "Dear Jeenie: Or should I say Barnabas? Thanks for the great encouragement of your letter. . . ."

Barnabas is not a biblical person we know as well as Peter, James, John, or Paul. He is rather obscure, actually, but his claim to fame was that he was an encourager. All the time. Constantly.

Here are some ways to be an encourager to your kids:

- *Encourage by spending quantity and quality time with your teenager.* We've heard for a long time about quality time. That's good. But kids need lots of time as well. Be with your kids—physically and emotionally.
- *Encourage them not to take themselves so seriously.* They need to give themselves a break on occasion. Lighten up.
- *Encourage them to develop a grateful heart.* Hans Selye, a brilliant scientist, believed one of the best ways to reduce stress is to have a grateful heart. In other words, quit bellyaching and be thankful. "A tranquil heart is life to the body," says Proverbs 14:30.
- *Encourage them to practice happiness.* Laugh a lot. It's good for what ails you. Solomon proclaims in Proverbs 17:22, "A joyful heart is good medicine, but a broken spirit dries up the bones."

Positive Results of Good Self-Esteem

Children who develop positive self-esteem will be more assertive rather than overbearing. They will be able to tell others what they need, set boundaries to protect the good things in their life while shutting out the bad, and be honest with themselves and others.

They will be more willing to take risks to venture into new areas of life—not the kind where they drag race all around town. The fear of failure will be less pronounced. Yet they will learn in order to succeed, they must, at times, accept defeat.

Life will become more enjoyable because they are honest, are willing to try new things, curtail complaining, express and savor their curiosity and exuberance, appreciate good relationships while treasuring the zest of just being alive.

Who knows, positive self-regard may rub off on the whole clan!

Coming to Grips

1. List five strengths of each of your children.
   a. ______________________________
   b. ______________________________
   c. ______________________________
   d. ______________________________
   e. ______________________________

2. Sit down with each child and discuss his or her strengths.

3. List three ways you can build your teen's self-esteem. Write a plan for working on each area.
   a. ______________________________
   b. ______________________________
   c. ______________________________

4. Refer to the section titled "Setting Appropriate Boundaries" and list the ones on which you can improve. Give ways in which you want to accomplish your goal.
   a. ______________________________
   b. ______________________________
   c. ______________________________

12

Letting Go Just Ain't Easy

In transferring the reins of authority (the rudiments of power) to your children, the task should be completed by twenty years and no later than twenty-two years of age. To hold on longer is to invite revolution.

James Dobson, *Parenting Isn't for Cowards*

Economics, in particular, have held today's adult children at home longer than previous generations. Finding a goodpaying job isn't easy; college is expensive; and paying for an apartment is costly. The age of marriage has also risen, keeping many adult children living with their parents. There is also a prevalent desire among parents (particularly mothers) to keep their offspring in the home as long as possible—to make life easy for them.

Overprotection

Overprotection tends to keep adults living under Mom and Dad's roof too long.

She was a petite, graying grandmother who came into my office following her urgent telephone call for help. Both she and her husband were looking forward to solitude and the enjoyment of retirement years. However, their lives were constantly interrupted by a renegade son who repeatedly came back home. Not only did he return, but he brought along his four kids.

"I don't know what's wrong with our son," the mother expressed. "He has been in and out of jail as a drug dealer, and now his sixteen-year-old girlfriend is pregnant. She's the age of his daughter. He won't work, and we're trying to support our four grandchildren as well as our son. It takes all the money we can get together just to survive.

"Today we learned he steals at night to buy drugs, accompanied by our two teenage grandchildren. We're just sick. We don't know what to do."

"How old is your son?" I asked.

"Thirty-nine," she replied.

"It sounds like it's been a swinging door to your home for years," I responded. "He has free lodging, food, and care for his children—with no responsibility. It's time to end it."

There were deep lines of weariness etched into her face, dark circles under her eyes, and a look of hopelessness. She was a pretty woman, well-groomed, and gentle. Too gentle! Sorrowfully, this mother looked at me and asked, "What should I do?"

"Throw them out," was my reply.

You would have thought I had taken a shotgun and sprayed her with bullets. Her face registered shock, it seemed as though her body was collapsing, her breathing became labored, and tears welled up in her dark eyes.

Mustering what little strength was available, she said, "Oh, I just couldn't. They would starve."

"They may miss a meal or two," I replied, "and probably need to live in their car for a while, but they won't *die*. It's time for your son to become a man and take responsibility for providing for his family.

"How long will you allow this to go on?" I continued. "Until he's forty-five? He will not change until you exhibit some tough love actions. It will be painful for you but healthy for your son and his children. The entire family must learn the value of work and self-provision."

As she rose to leave, she hugged me. "You're right. I'm going to tell my husband what you have said, and I hope we have the courage to follow through."

Granted, this appears to be an unusual case. However, I've seen other such scenarios. Why do parents protect their children from taking care of themselves? What has happened to the *work ethic* in our society?

Over and over students tell me, "My parents do not want me to work. They want me to get good grades." Yet these same parents buy brand-new cars for their teenagers, supply insurance and gasoline, while the adolescents are speeding and careening their hot vehicles all over town, having the carefree time of their lives.

I see rescuing going on—big time.

When we over-give to our children, we teach them to be unappreciative. They learn they can have about anything their hearts desire. There are few consequences to their behavior because someone will fix it for them. Children who are indulged will never have "enough." Their desires are insatiable—their appreciation nonexistent. Are these the future citizens we want to raise?

Deparenting

Thankfully, there is a healthy, supportive manner to help our children start out on their own. When do we begin to deparent? At age two.

Here's a helpful slogan: "Don't do anything for your children that they can do for themselves." Children can do many things for themselves. By the time they are teenagers, they need to have learned basic survival skills and be ready to meet the outside world relatively well prepared.

When our children are grown, our role must change from parent to friend. Granted, they will always be our children and we their parents; however, the healthy relationship is one in which the transition has changed from child/adult to adult/adult. Having our children as adult friends is incredibly satisfying, freeing, and rewarding.

Some parents are determined to rule their offspring. Forever. Adult children who are still controlled by their parents tend to feel obligated to visit, frequently telephone, and meet the wishes of their parents. There are a lot of *shoulds* and *have tos* in their thinking and vocabulary. The umbilical cord is not completely severed.

Prior to birth, the umbilical cord is life-giving. It allows freedom while providing protection, nurturing, and sustenance. In childhood it is more like a bungee cord—giving a little room to explore, then bringing the child back to home base. By adulthood, the cord must be cut to allow for a two-way strand of love. Connection without restrictions.

One way of deparenting is through *healthy role models*. Encourage your child in supplementary loving relationships with family, close friends, and trustworthy adults. As the child grows, he or she can experience healthy bonding.

Over the years, I've built a bond with my nieces. It began when they were little kids.

Picking up the phone, I asked my brother, "Why don't you put the girls on the plane a few days before you drive down for the holidays. I'll pick them up at the airport and treat them to Disneyland."

Two excited little girls (ages four and seven) bounded from the airplane into my arms—squealing. "I have a surprise for you tomorrow morning," I promised.

Pulling into the parking lot the next day, the older one yelled, "Disneyland!" I had the joy of escorting them on their first trip to the Magic Kingdom.

During the ensuing years, I've telephoned them, mailed letters of encouragement—sometimes with cookies (while in college). Always with love. Now, as young adults, there exists a loving bond.

Often during the teenage years, it is difficult for parent and child to talk on a variety of issues. We parents are terrified of our children getting into drugs, alcohol, sex (to name a few), which makes it very difficult to separate our emotions in order to have a logical talk.

Many parents have commented that their son or daughter appreciates and accepts my advice. Yet what their parents say seems to go in one ear and out the other. Usually, I've said nothing different than what the parent has been saying for years. However, since I am not responsible for their outcome, I can step aside from the emotional involvement. Sometimes, during the adolescent years, kids are more willing to listen to other adults whom they respect.

Our children need additional direction from people who can be trusted. Hopefully, as parents, we have encouraged them to cultivate this supplementary source, even though we are still number one in their life.

Increased responsibility is another way to deparent. It is surprising how many teens do not know how to launder clothes, cook, manicure a lawn, clean house, balance a checkbook, or keep a budget.

We render them a great disservice if we shove them into a cold, cruel world without survival skills. It's our privilege and responsibility to teach our children how to cope in the adult world.

Living with Adult Children

In past generations, boys learned to do the work of a man. Girls were taught homemaking skills. Even though many married in their teens and early twenties, they were well prepared to begin their own homes.

Today, marriage is delayed. By the time the wedding occurs, the bride and groom have been adults for a number of years. Yet many still live at home until the nuptials transpire.

"As long as he lives under my roof," one father bellowed, "he is going to obey my rules. It's my way or the highway."

"What rules do you have in mind for your twenty-five-year-old son?" I questioned.

Just as I thought. They were the *same* rules as when his adult child was an adolescent (prior to age eighteen). The father did not look on his offspring as an adult.

Problems arise when parents expect adult children to continue to obey restrictions from their adolescent years. I fully understand that eighteen-year-olds are not adults *emotionally*. However, the laws of our land state that they are *legally* of age and are treated as such by the authorities.

My heart almost leaped out of my chest as I fumbled to turn on a lamp and grope for the telephone at 2:00 in the morning.

"Do you know where Kathi is?" the male voice asked. "I called her dorm, and no one knows anything. I'm worried about her."

At that information, my heart really began to pound. The young man she was dating was concerned enough to call me. "No," I responded, trying desperately to think if she had told me where she was going. Racking my brain did no good. I had no idea where she could be at 2:00 A.M.

After he hung up, I felt panic. My mind went crazy, vividly depicting all kinds of horrid scenarios. I quietly prayed for God's protection. In about half an hour, I called the college dorm. Kathi was there.

"Mom, we had the most wonderful time. A bunch of us girls decided we needed to do something fun. So we took off for Disneyland and stayed until it closed at midnight. We were in such a crazy mood, we decided to go out to eat. We drove a long way to find this super restaurant. It was great. We just got in," my daughter enthusiastically reported.

Thank God, I thought. Relief!

Here is my advice on rules for an adult child.

1. Restrictions should be no different than they would be for any other unmarried adult guest in your home. For instance: I would not allow premarital sex, drugs, or alcohol in my home by any adult. This would be agreed upon at the beginning. No confusion.

2. Housemates need to show common courtesy to each other by leaving a note as to where they will be and the approximate time of return (if gone an extended length of time). If you notice, I said nothing about *curfew*. An adult child at home is just that—an adult. He or she is responsible for his or her hours and where he or she chooses to go.

3. I would not pay for a roommate's car, upkeep, or insurance. Neither should a parent. The adult child is the total caretaker of his or her car needs. In order to save

money, it can be a wise choice to have the adult child's car on the family insurance policy. However, the adult child should pay the premium.

"My adult son has a good job, yet he has not paid for his car insurance for nine months," one mother bemoaned. "I don't know how to get the money. He promises but never comes through."

"Delete his car from the policy after a one-month warning," I encouraged.

By the look on the mother's face, it was apparent she would probably continue to pay—then complain.

4. If I rented out a room, I would not provide laundry service or cook meals. Your adult child needs to do all his or her own laundry—or choose to wear dirty apparel. The care of an adult's clothes is his or her obligation.

When I lived in the college dorm, there was a young man who mailed his laundry home. It must have cost a bundle to send dirty clothes from California to Michigan. Mom would launder, iron, and package them up for a return trip.

For the live-in adult child, the mother may choose to cook family meals. However, if the adult child is not there for the mealtimes, he or she must fend for himself or herself.

A distressed mother called in to the radio talk-show psychologist: "My son is twenty-two," she stated. "He doesn't have a job, nor does he want one. He sleeps until noon and runs around all night with his buddies. When he gets in about 3:00 in the morning, I listen for his car and get up to fix dinner for him."

Needless to say, the therapist was irritated and tried to talk sense to this doting parent. It was difficult for Mom to allow her son to become accountable for his life.

After I spoke at a seminar, a father approached me. "My son is thirty-three. He owns his own business, and it was doing badly, so he moved home for a few months. That was four years ago. Now his business is going great guns—has been for several years."

"How much rent is he paying?" I quizzed.

"Oh, I wouldn't want to charge him anything. I have to pay for it anyway, so it's nothing extra out of my pocket. Besides, he mows the lawn."

My, my. This adult child really gets off easy. No expenses—just pushes the lawnmower around once a week for an hour.

I'm a great believer in charging rent (even if you're a millionaire). Check the newspapers for the going rate, and ask a little less. Or work out a specific agreement for work done in lieu of part of the rent, then deduct the amount you would pay for hiring outside help.

Often parents are distraught because their adult child is on drugs, won't work, lies around the house, and expects complete maid service. "How can I get him/her to move out?" they ask.

"Keep raising the rent," is my response. "Eventually, the adult child will say, 'Hey, I can get an apartment for what you're charging me.' With a sly grin, offer to help him or her pack."

The numbers are rising of adult children in their late twenties who are living in their parents' home rent free and without obligations. They are learning life need not have liabilities, hard times, nor responsibilities.

When Leaving Home Is a Difficult Choice

If your child lies around all day, runs around all night, refuses to pay rent or work for his or her keep, it's time to have a heart-to-heart talk. Something like:

"Son (or daughter), we realize we're doing you a disservice by allowing you to be dependent on us. We want you to become a person who has self-respect and is responsible for himself.

"In three months (give the exact date), you will be expected to move into your own place. We hope you will have a job by then and a place to live. However, if you don't, we will still insist on your leaving.

"We will give you $_______ to help with your first month's rent and groceries. After that, you will be on your own.

"Depend on us to pray for you every day and to be emotionally available. We believe in you."

Some adult children are confident the parent will not follow through. A number of them, after having lived a few days in their car, quickly learn that a job and a roof over their head is *their* responsibility.

The Living-at-Home College Student

Getting a college education, and particularly living on campus, costs megabucks today. Because of the financial hardship, many parents prefer their adult child live at home. If the student is full-time (twelve or more credits) with at least a C average (2.0), I think it is acceptable to provide *free* room and board.

Just because a student lives at home, however, does not mean he or she cannot hold down a part-time job (full-time in summer). All his or her personal expenses (clothes, entertainment, car payments, gas, insurance, repairs) need to be met out of his or her paycheck. By working, a student can easily earn enough to pay for his or her books and a percentage of his or her tuition.

The Student Who Lives on Campus

In this setting, the college costs become exorbitant. Yet there are many plans to finance education.

When their children were preschoolers, one set of parents built a lakeside cabin—doing most of the work themselves. Their intent was to make yearly improvements, then sell the cabin when their children entered college. The money from the sale would finance the entire college costs including room and board.

The time came to put the lakeside cabin up for sale. Once again the parents strolled along the thickly wooded pathways, enjoyed the relaxing sound of the water gently lapping on the shore, breathed in the toxin-free air, listened to the wind blowing through the multi-colored leaves, cuddled up to a warm fireplace in a room where memories and laughter were deeply etched into the walls. The for-sale sign came down.

They went to plan B. They chose to put a second mortgage on their home, took on additional employment (one evening a week), encouraged their children to work part-time, and subsidized with scholarships.

Things do not always go as we have planned, but there are alternate strategies that can eventually bring us to the desired goal.

"With our girls," one father explained, "we had several aspirations in regard to their college education:

1. We wanted them to leave home and go to college out of the area. We believed this would help bring about maturity and growth.
2. Living on campus was important, as was attending the same college four years. It would enable them to be incorporated into a community and feel they were an integral part.

3. Going to a Christian college was vital. We had a list of colleges we believed were educationally sound and spiritually based from which they could choose.
4. Because we chose to finance most of the education, we believed it to be our *scholarship award* to them; therefore, the dollars were not without a few stipulations."

This couple encouraged their daughters to pursue academic scholarships in high school, as well as earn money in the summers toward their education. The pre-agreement was:

1. Except for books and personal expenses, all costs (tuition, food, housing) would be paid by the parents the *first* year.
2. The next three years, the parents would pay the same original dollar amount. Any tuition increase would be picked up by the student.
3. If the adult child lost her scholarship because of grades, she would make up the difference.

"Our plan has been a difficult decision, and sometimes I think I should have contributed more. It's hard to know what is fair," mused the father.

Forming a plan is critical, yet knowing exactly which course is equitable is not easy. The line between being a healthy supporter versus an overprotector is hazy.

Recently, I plowed through over forty applications of needy students. Here are some of the things scholarship committees consider before awarding money:

1. Does the student have other scholarships/grants? What is the amount?

2. Are there government loans to be repaid after graduation? How many?
3. How much money does the student need?
4. Does the student work? How many hours per week?
5. What year is the student?
6. What is the G.P.A. (grade point average)? Is it 2.5 or better?
7. Is he or she a full-time student (twelve or more credits)?
8. Are the parents able to help with college costs?

My heart went out to those students as I vividly recalled my days of college poverty. Reading through the applications, I wanted to give them all big hunks of scholarship money. However, I chose larger scholarship awards for those students who were holding down a job, getting decent grades, and had applied for other available scholarships.

As a parent, check out colleges several years prior to your child attending. Look at tuition, housing, and books, as well as additional fees, which can add greatly to the cost. Make an appointment with the financial aid officer to check on packages the college offers, as well as state and federal loans and grants. If you apply for state and federal loans, the parent will be assessed a contribution dollar amount in accord with your yearly income, number of dependents, and net worth. Contact banks who make student loans and inquire as to interest fees and payback schedule. Look closely at your financial status and decide how much you are able to contribute yearly.

Discuss the financial plan with your student early in the junior year of high school. Also, address your goals for your child's financial involvement (scholarships, working). Insist that your offspring apply for scholarships through the high school. Thousands of scholarship dollars go unawarded each year because of lack of applicants. Even though many scholarships are in $100 and $200 amounts, they add up quickly and are generally renewed yearly.

Leaving Home—the Healthy Way

We raise our kids to leave home. Eventually. It is our responsibility to help them exit as intact, stable, sturdy, and competent as possible.

We prepare them to go to kindergarten, be vaccinated, visit the dentist, bury a beloved pet. Yet seldom do we formulate a plan to launch them into an independent life.

From the time she was a small child, I raised my daughter with the idea of her living on the campus of a Christian college. One sunny August morning, we made the trek to the college of her choice. As we unloaded the car and carried endless boxes into her room, my mind escaped to another Saturday years earlier when I, too, as a teenager had moved into a dorm. The excitement was exhilarating, yet mixed with sadness in leaving home, with uncertainty of a new adventure, and with timidity in making new friends. Bittersweet.

Now, at the other end of the spectrum, I viewed the move from parental eyes—excitement for my daughter, hope she would continue to make good decisions, enthusiasm for her choice of a fine college, anticipation of her personal and academic growth, and the joy of new experiences college life would bring. Yet, as a single parent, my awareness of a new aloneness filled my eyes with tears as I drove away.

For three years Kathi lived in the dorm during the school term, coming home during vacation breaks. Near the end of her junior year, she began thinking about moving into an apartment with friends (an off-campus complex of upperclassmen) for her senior year. During her last summer at home, we often talked about her upcoming move.

"I think this will be a wonderful move for you," I said. "You have been increasing your independence, and I believe you are ready to be on your own. I have great confidence you will do well with complete autonomy. I believe in you. However, now that you are an adult, my responsibility to God for you has ended. My new obligation is to pray for you daily, to listen, and to be supportive. Count on me for that."

By the end of the summer, Kathi was emotionally ready to launch out on her own.

The Art of Being an Encourager

Once your adult child has moved out, fight off your impulses to reinstate the old parent/child roles. Instead, learn to be your child's encouraging friend.

Listen to your adult child. Try to remember how it feels to be young, on your own, dealing with adult responsibilities, and uncertain. Be accessible.

Give advice only when asked. Suppress the desire to be in control or tell your adult child more than he or she wants to know. On occasion, he or she will ask for your input. At that point: (1) Send up a silent prayer for wisdom. (2) Say it only *once*.

Offer occasional help. One of the less threatening ways to help is to take your adult child grocery shopping. State a dollar amount you're willing to spend, then let him or her enjoy the trip, and don't spoil it by critiquing his or her choices. Or, if you know what he or she needs, take over a bag of groceries. Clean out your pantry, and donate food you won't be using. When your adult child comes to dinner, send home leftovers.

A fond memory from the poverty years of my early marriage was receiving a package of pork chops from my mother-in-law. I was thrilled.

Loaning money can become complicated. One way is to graciously loan the money and ask for a check in return. Have your adult child postdate the check, and hold it for a short time. This system allows the parent to be magnanimous, while keeping it as a business transaction.

Gifts, now and then, are a real treat. Meet a special need or wish. Enjoy giving, and watch the delight of receiving. A word of caution: Give with no strings attached or expectations in return—even excessive gratitude.

Visitation rights. You are a guest. Don't pop in unannounced. Respect your adult child's privacy to be a separate individual.

Live a little. Now that you have raised your kids, it's time to catch up on all the things you have always wanted to do. Savor the fruits of your labor. Get out there and enjoy life.

In Closing

Recently I attended a professional workshop by therapist Chris Rubel, who stated, "Children are born into a wonderful relationship, trash it, then leave."

Sometimes. More often, adult children are very grateful for their parents' sacrifice and love.

Years ago, my daughter wrote a special note. I carried it in my wallet until it was well worn, then I put it in my memory box. I sorted through two large boxes of keepsake mementos, hunting for this particular note. In the search, I found many notes of love and appreciation from her, as well as the one I wanted to quote.

Several years after college graduation, Kathi was using her sociology degree in a low-paying, government-funded job. Though it was rewarding, money worries were her constant companion. Her note read:

> Mom, you didn't need to give me that money, but it sure does help. "And my God shall supply. . . ." I don't know

> why that's the verse I most often forget when I most need to remember it!
>
> Mom, I love you *so* much. I am ever so grateful to the Lord for allowing me to glimpse his love through you. You are my "most biggest" blessing.

If we adequately prepare our kids to leave, then let them go, we will always have them!

Coming to Grips

1. Ask yourself, "What scares me the most about letting go?"
   a. __________
   b. __________
   c. __________
   d. __________

2. In the above list, which ones are unfounded fears? Put an *F* (for fear) beside them.

3. In what ways can my child be better prepared for an independent life?
   a. __________
   b. __________
   c. __________

4. Write down a plan to ready your child for life away from home.
   a. __________
   b. __________
   c. __________
   d. __________
   e. __________

Follow the Leader

Remember the childhood game of "Follow the Leader"? Whoever was lucky enough to be the leader would steer the entourage over hill and dale while performing antics gleaned from a vivid imagination. We carefully imitated each minute detail because we wanted to be certain when it was our turn to lead that we, too, could feel the surge of power as we charted an exciting course for the neighborhood crew.

In a sense, we are all followers—and leaders. Like it or not, there are people who emulate our examples. Especially our kids.

In the Old Testament, we have a multitude of illustrations of ghastly kings. The monarchs were cruel, arrogant, and literally shook their fists in the face of the God of Israel. So did their sons, grandsons, and great-grandsons. Generation upon generation patterned their lives after their godless ancestors.

Then there were David, Samuel, Hezekiah, Moses, Joseph, and Josiah. Godly men. Leaders who chose to follow Jehovah—closely. Their lives were exemplary—godly models that could be followed.

How we choose to live will make an enormous impact on our kids. Good or bad.

Teenagers often act as though they could not care less about the values and input of their parents. However, it is not the way they truly feel. Numerous studies have found adolescents to highly value their parents' beliefs and standards, and parents have more influence over their children than do their peers. After counseling with thousands of teenagers, I concur with these findings.

Modeling the Good Stuff

When I mess up big time, I hope no one has been following my example. It's not easy to be a prototype. However, with our children, we are continual models.

Parents often catch their preschoolers in the act of mimicking Mom and Dad—perfectly. Same mannerisms. Exact tone of voice. Many a chagrined parent has vowed to be different after seeing a mirror image of himself or herself.

Let's look at some of the behaviors we demonstrate.

Loyalty

A female client was furious because her husband constantly cut down family and friends behind their backs, and sometimes to their faces. "My parents drilled into me, 'If you can't say anything good, don't say anything at all,'" she expressed.

Sure hit home with me. I thought about the times I should have kept my mouth shut. So I'm practicing. I'm trying to either keep quiet or respond with a considerate remark. When I discipline myself in this regard, I feel so much better about my willingness to grow.

It's important to be a loyal friend and family member and to defend rather than degrade. When our kids hear us demean the people we love, it gives them license to do the same.

Respect

A lot of things deserve respect. Our country, church, boss/employees, pastor, flag—to name a few. Unless we show respect by what we say and do, our kids will not prize or internalize our values.

Ever notice the guy at a ball game *sitting* during the national anthem and flag ceremony? A hot dog is balanced on his belly, he has a beer in one hand, his body is slopped all over the seat, and he's burping. His kid is watching him closely, and in a few years, Junior will probably act just like Dad.

More than one teenager has turned away from God and the church because his or her parent had no respect for the pastor, church board, or most members. All the kid heard was criticism. Years later, the parent wonders why in the world the teen refuses to go to church.

Honesty

We can be truly honest yet uncritical. Sounds paradoxical. Criticism can be scathing truth, no holds barred, unkind, and without regard for a person's feelings. Conversely, we can confront issues honestly, yet sincerely, by using "I" messages.

> "My feelings were hurt, and I need to talk to you about it. I felt betrayed when you remained silent as Bar-

bara gave all the gory details of how I lost my job. As my friend, I wanted you to come to my defense."

With this type of confrontation, a response from your friend might be:

"I feel awful I let you down. When it was happening, I was embarrassed and didn't know what to say. I value our friendship, and I'm truly sorry."

The key to confronting is to work it out.

An important part of honesty has to do with *telling the truth*. My mom raised the three of us to believe lying was just about the worst thing in the world. Consequently, I have lied only a few times in my life. They are etched in my memory because I had to humbly go to the persons and make it right. The recollection of confession is so horrible, it keeps me on the straight and narrow.

Most teenage students would almost rather I catch them in the act of murder, it seems, than a lie. Believe me, when a kid lies to me, I come totally unglued—I get enraged. The majority of adolescents tell me the truth. Guess the word has gotten around.

"*Everyone* lies," someone recently told me. I hope not.

Let's examine lying. There are the bold-faced, outright lies; then, there are the tiny white ones. Or so people want to believe. Truth is, there just ain't no color to lies. They're all the same—wrong.

"Tell them I'm not home," yells Dad to his child who is holding the phone. Dad doesn't want to talk to the caller, so he asks the child to lie for him. Hmmm.

An honest response would be, "Tell him (or her) I'm unable to come to the phone right now, but I will call back at a later time." (Then do it.) Or, if it's a solicitation, the reply could be: "Tell them I am not interested in their product."

Two things the child will learn: (1) It is important to respond honestly. (2) Kindness is vital.

Cheating is another form of untruthfulness. Defrauding Uncle Sam is common. Believe me, it's crossed my mind. I was caught in a complex web when a limited partnership went bankrupt and all of the investors were left holding the bag. The IRS collected thousands of dollars in interest and penalties from me.

I'll never forget the look on my four-year-old daughter's face as she intently listened to my conversation in a store. I had lugged the coffee urn to the cash register. As the clerk rang up the merchandise, I realized it was mismarked—lower. A lot.

"This price is incorrect," I said. "The sign said it was $______." The cashier called the manager. He profusely thanked me for my honesty and said I could have the product at the lesser price.

As we wound our way toward the car, I explained to my daughter why I called attention to the mistake. Because I chose to be honest, I was rewarded by getting the coffee pot at a much lower price without the guilt of cheating.

"Hey, I got this great sweater for twenty bucks," an acquaintance bragged.

"Wow!" I exclaimed. "It looks like a very expensive sweater."

"It was," he responded, "but the dingbat clerk gave me the wrong change. She'll probably lose her job over that one."

I was appalled and told him so.

"That's her problem," he exclaimed. "If she's that stupid, she deserves it."

We're all tempted to lie and cheat and have probably succumbed at one time or another. But we cannot expect our children to be honest if we model dishonesty.

Consistency

People who can't be counted on drive me nuts. Most people in my life do what they promise. When we plan to meet at a certain time, I can be sure they will be there within five minutes. If it goes longer, I realize there has either been a miscommunication or something has happened over which they had no control.

I've known others who are notorious for being late, making everyone wait, or not showing up at all. This pattern is highly disrespectful and a selfish way of life.

Children *trust* parents. They count on what a parent says. To a child, it's an oath.

Looking into the sad brown eyes of a young divorced mother, I listened as she said, "I got my little ones ready for their daddy. They were so excited, they sat on the porch for an hour waiting. Then two hours. He never came. Their little hearts were broken, and they couldn't understand why Daddy didn't come. I held them in my arms and rocked them until the tears stopped and sleep quieted their pain. I could have killed him."

What a sad picture of little ones who trusted a father who was undependable.

Teenagers also feel the sting of parents who do not take their promises seriously.

"My mom and dad have never come to one of my games," a junior football hero said. The tears began to well as he continued, "They promised me over and over they would be there, but I know they will never come. So there's no reason to play football in my senior year." No amount of encouragement and coaxing from either me or his coach would convince this young football star to continue on the team his senior year. More of Gino's story is told in chapter 6.

Occasionally, we will make a rash commitment or an unavoidable circumstance will not allow us to honor our pledge. Kids understand and forgive the atypical. My concern is over *consistent inconsistencies*—a lifestyle that tells your adolescent loud and clear that he or she doesn't matter enough for you to follow through on what was promised.

Choose to be a parent on whom your child can rely.

Having Fun

So, are you fun to live with? Most of us aren't sure. "Sometimes, I guess," some would answer. Others shrug their shoulders and roll their eyes.

Home needs to be a fun place. We get caught up in the web of daily living—bills, cleaning, mail, laundry, shopping, telephone calls, lawns, errands, cooking, chauffeuring, car upkeep. The list is nearly endless. Stuff that is just plain drudgery for the most part. Not much fun. Yet, these are things that must be done to keep life running fairly smoothly.

Fun needs to be written into our schedule. Too bad it's that way, but it is. Unless we *plan* merriment into our lives, it isn't likely to occur very often. When I speak of fun, I don't mean going to the expensive amusement parks where we spend all day and half the night shelling out megabucks. Most satisfying pleasures are free and simple.

There is a delightful verse that says, "A joyful heart is good medicine" (Prov. 17:22). One of the best things we can do for our emotions, our bodies, and our souls is to laugh. I attended a three-day conference a few years ago on *laughter*. Never had I realized the physical, emotional, and spiritual importance of rollicking humor. Keep the family spirits up with merriment.

In my book to teenagers, *If My Parents Are Getting Divorced, Why Am I the One Who Hurts?*, I listed some ideas for having a fun-filled home:

- The entire family can be birthday angels for a week before the birthday. Each birthday angel does nice things for the person who is having a birthday. For instance, a family member sees an unmade bed. So he or she makes it and puts a little piece of paper on the pillow that simply says, "From your birthday angel." The birthday angel constantly looks for ways in which he or she can be kind and considerate. During this time, the birthday person will feel loved, appreciated, and special as an air of excitement permeates the house.
- At Christmas, have each member draw a name and become a Christmas angel two weeks before Christmas.
- I'm a great believer in little practical jokes. All kinds of funny things can bring merriment to a home. It's critical, however, that no joke is malicious or damaging.
- Playing made-up games is also great fun. One time I began a game with the sentence, "I'm grateful for the time I never got caught when I . . ." As each family member finished the sentence and wove his or her yarn, the tales became wild and crazy. We also learned a lot about each other.
- Drawing names for a secret pal is fun. This can be for a more extended period of time (maybe three months). Rules need to be set, such as:

1. The secret pal must be in touch once a week.
2. Little or no money is to be involved.
3. It will go from June 1 through August 31.
4. On August 31, the secret pals will be revealed at a family party.

- We once read a long, hilarious Christmas play called *The Best Christmas Pageant Ever,* by Barbara Robinson. It's a tale about the wild and unruly Herdman family, who hadn't a clue of what the Christmas story was about. They cussed their teachers, talked dirty, hit, lied, and smoked. The whole church was shocked when they wanted to play all the major roles in the Christmas pageant. Their antics make a delightful play. We passed the book from person to person, and it took all afternoon to read the story aloud. But what a memorable, lively, and amusing time.
- Long before Pictionary became a real game (manufactured and marketed), we made up our own. Still do.

These are a few ideas that can help you get started on having an enjoyable home life. Having fun keeps a family close. When we play together, we are less afraid to be honest. And when the tough times come, we are more willing to support each other.

The Media

More than any other time in history, the media (in a variety of forms) surrounds, compels, and dictates our lives. Television is probably number one. According to James Dobson in *Children at Risk,* one study states the average high school student has watched eighteen thousand murders on T.V. Another statistic informs us that children sixteen to eighteen years old will spend fifteen thousand hours watching T.V. compared with thirteen thousand hours in school.

What we parents watch will have great influence on our kids, as well as what we allow them to see. Turning off the tube isn't easy. I've sat through many a show I didn't like, shouldn't have been watching, or was bored with just because I was too lazy to turn the thing off.

Movies are a strong second. I am very cautious about what I view, since it's very easy to build a tolerance for sex and violence. We hardly notice anymore. If we want our children to see wholesome films, then we had better adhere to a similar guideline. Kids watch what we do.

Sometimes I fear we're losing some of the really good things in life—for instance, excellent, time-honored books and classical music. Many teens have not had a great deal of exposure to timeless literature and music. "It's boring," they complain.

Some teachers play classical music while students study or do their assignments. I've seen it at the elementary level as well as in high school. When I walk into the classroom, the students are quiet, calm, relaxed, and working hard. Eventually, kids can begin to appreciate and acquire a taste for the music of yesteryear.

A friend described her family's Christmas Eve custom. "We put the *Nutcracker* CD on, then pass out instruments to all the kids (cymbals, triangles, sticks, bells, tambourine). During Tchaikovsky's piece, the 'conductor' points to the various instruments, and the orchestra members follow his or her lead. Afterwards, we open presents." What a unique idea.

When we read trashy books and listen only to contemporary music, our children will not be exposed to more diverse forms of expression. Variety is the spice of life, and education is meant to be broadening. There is a wide range of worthwhile books and music to be explored. I encourage you to expand your horizons and stretch out the borders. Your kids will be more apt to follow suit.

Cleaning Up Our Mouths

"Get this blinkety-blank kid out of my classroom!" a teacher screamed into the phone.

The student sheepishly entered my office and handed me the discipline referral, which stated, "Eric used profanity in class."

Excuse me! I thought. *The audacity of the teacher yelling curse words into the telephone as forty students listened, then sending an adolescent to be disciplined for the same thing.*

We can't expect kids to clean up their mouths if they hear swearing from teachers and parents. Some parents excuse it with, "Well, I only swear when I'm mad." Our society has grown progressively worse in the area of foul language and blasphemy. Even though the words may pass through our minds on occasion, it's imperative they do not escape our lips.

When I hear kids cuss out their parents, I get livid. So often, the parent hardly notices. But I do. I will not allow a student to talk disrespectfully to *anyone* in my presence. If they do, they regret it.

Giving of Ourselves and Our Time

Giving of our time and energy to our family is not easy in this rat-race world.

In the 1970s there was a popular song by Harry Chapin called "Cats in the Cradle." It told the story of a little boy who desperately wanted his father to do things with him. But Dad was busy making a living and always promised a future date, stating "We'll have a good time then, son."

The expectant, patient young lad grew up and began a life and family of his own. His retired father now had time for his son, but the tables were turned. The adult son exhibited the same behavior so carefully modeled by his father in earlier years. Never available. Always promising, "We'll have a good time then, Dad."

A sad scenario.

In order to be a noteworthy model to our children, we need to be with them enough to be an example. If our kids rarely see us or have little communication of substance, our values won't pack much of a wallop.

Former First Lady Barbara Bush, in a commencement address on June 1, 1990, to Wellesley College graduates, said: "As important as your obligations as a doctor, lawyer, or business leader will be, you are a human being first, and those human connections—with spouses, with children, with friends—are the most important investments you will ever make. At the end of your life you will never regret not having passed one more test, not winning one more verdict, or not closing one more deal. You will regret time not spent with a husband, a friend, a child, or a parent."

How true!

Modeling Godliness

My long-ago deceased mother (to whom this book is dedicated) was one of the most godly women I've known. She knew how to pray, commune with her Father, and bombard heaven.

When she went into the bedroom to spend time with her Lord, it was totally off limits to us three kids. "Unless the house is burning down or someone is dying, don't call me," was her warning.

Often I could hear the gentle murmurings of her intense prayer as I stood by her bedroom door. It seemed as though the glory and presence of the Lord escaped through the cracks. Mom knew how to touch God. She lived a life totally dedicated to Christ. No one has spiritually impacted my life to such a degree. She modeled Jesus to me.

In Closing

If we want our children to follow our leadership, then how we live our lives is vital. May God give us just plain guts to be exemplary. As Anne Ortlund says in *Disciplines of the Home*, "A Christian home is a powerful show-and-tell."

Coming to Grips

If we want our kids to follow our leadership, we need to be aware of how we are leading.

1. Check off these items to see how you are doing.

	good	okay	not so great
respect and loyalty	☐	☐	☐
honesty	☐	☐	☐
consistency	☐	☐	☐
fun loving	☐	☐	☐
decent T.V. shows	☐	☐	☐
wholesome movies	☐	☐	☐
good music	☐	☐	☐
fine books	☐	☐	☐
giving quantity/quality time	☐	☐	☐
godliness	☐	☐	☐

2. Now list the four areas at which you are the best:
   a. ____
   b. ____
   c. ____
   d. ____

3. Write three that need improvement:
   a. ____
   b. ____
   c. ____

Bibliography

Antonio, Gene. *The AIDS Cover-Up?* San Francisco: Ignatius Press, 1986.
Arterburn, Stephen, and Jim Burns. *Drug Proof Your Kids*. Colorado Springs: Focus on the Family Publishing, 1989.
———. *Steering Them Straight* (previously *When Love Is Not Enough*). Colorado Springs: Focus on the Family Publishing, 1996.
Bodenhammer, Greg. *Back in Control*. New York: Fireside and Colophon, 1992.
CARE Systems (Jack Woolworth), P.O. Box 964, Orange, CA 92666.
Dobson, James. *Hide or Seek*. Old Tappan, N.J.: Fleming H. Revell, 1979.
———. *Parenting Isn't for Cowards*. Dallas: Word, 1987.
Dobson, James, and Gary L. Bauer. *Children at Risk*. Dallas: Word, 1990.
Durfield, Richard, and Renee Durfield. *Raising Them Chaste*. Minneapolis: Bethany, 1991.
Gordon, Jeenie. *If My Parents Are Getting Divorced, Why Am I the One Who Hurts?* Grand Rapids: Zondervan, 1993.
Jenkins, Jerry. *As You Leave Home*. Colorado Springs: Focus on the Family Publishing, 1993.
Kesler, Jay. *Ten Mistakes Parents Make with Teenagers (and How to Avoid Them)*. Brentwood: Wolgemuth & Hyatt Publishers, 1988.
———. *Too Big to Spank*. Ventura, Calif.: Regal Books, 1978.
Kiersey, David, and Marilyn Bates. *Please Understand Me*. Delmar, Calif.: Prometheus Nemesis Books, 1978.
King, Paul. *Sex, Drugs & Rock 'n Roll*. Bellevue, Wash.: Professional Counselor Books, 1988.
McDowell, Josh. *It Can Happen to You*. Dallas: Word, 1991.
McDowell, Josh, and Dick Day. *Why Wait?* San Bernardino, Calif.: Here's Life Publishers, 1987.
Narramore, Bruce. *Adolescence Is Not an Illness*. Grand Rapids: Revell, 1991.

Ortlund, Anne. *Disciplines of the Home*. Dallas: Word, 1990.
Ridenour, Fritz. *What Teenagers Wish Their Parents Knew about Kids*. Dallas: Word, 1982.
Schimmels, Cliff. *Parents' Most-Asked Questions about Kids and Schools*. Wheaton: Victor, 1989.
Tough Love, P.O. Box 70, Sellersville, PA 18960.

Jeenie Gordon, a high school counselor for nineteen years, is a single parent, conference speaker, and the author of three books. She has appeared frequently on *Focus on the Family* and other radio broadcasts.

*If you make the Most High your dwelling—
even the Lord, who is my refuge—then no
harm will befall you, no disaster will
come near your tent.
For he will command his angels
concerning you to guard you in all your
ways; they will lift you up in their hands
so that you will not strike your foot agains
a stone. You will tread upon the lion and
the cobra; you will trample the great lion
and the serpent.
"Because he loves me," says the Lord,
"I will rescue him; I will protect him,
for he acknowledges my name.
He will call upon me, and I will answer
him;
I will be with him in trouble, I will
deliver him and honour him. With
long life will I satisfy him and show
him my salvation."

Psalm 91:9-16

FAITH: what it takes to
believe in anything unseen...
ex the wind, love, hope, trust, tomorrow